Radical Consumption

Radical Consumption

Shopping for change in contemporary culture

Jo Littler

 Open University Press

Open University Press
McGraw-Hill Education
McGraw-Hill House
Shoppenhangers Road
Maidenhead
Berkshire
England
SL6 2QL

email: enquiries@openup.co.uk
world wide web: www.openup.co.uk

and Two Penn Plaza, New York, NY 10121-2289, USA

First published 2009

A catalogue record of this book is available from the British Library

ISBN-13: 978-0-33-522152-3 (pb) 978-0-33-522153-0 (hb)
ISBN-10: 0-33-522152-1 (pb) 0-33-522153-X (hb)

Library of Congress Cataloging-in-Publication Data
CIP data applied for

Typeset by YHT Ltd, London
Printed in the UK by Bell and Bain Ltd., Glasgow

Fictitious names of companies, products, people, characters and/or data that may
be used herein (in case studies or in examples) are not intended to represent any
real individual, company, product or event.

The *McGraw·Hill* Companies

Contents

Acknowledgements

This book seems to have been a long time coming, and as I'm finishing it just before I'm due to give birth, I'd like to thank the squirming bundle of life inside of me for helping to finish it along.

Many other thanks are also due. One of the pleasures of academia, for me at least, are the connections and relationships made, both brief and long-lasting, through what Phil Agre calls different communities of interest. I am therefore grateful to all the people, conferences, spaces and places that helped me connect. Particular thanks to all those who invited me to give papers: Jim McGuigan and his colleagues at Loughborough (which made me rethink much of Chapter 1); Caroline Bassett and Janice Winship at the University of Sussex; Roberta Sassatelli for asking me along to a very interesting roundtable about alternative consumption at Birkbeck; and Clive Barnett and colleagues for asking me to participate in the excellent *Interdependence Day* event at the Royal Geographical Society. Thanks also to those who participated in the 'Cultural Studies and Anti-Consumerism' panels at Crossroads 2006, and to the contributors who wrote for the resultant issue of *Cultural Studies* (which taps into many themes of this book) as well as to Sam Binkley who co-edited that issue with me. I'm also grateful for the support of the British Academy for giving me an overseas conference travel grant, and to those at Middlesex who helped arrange teaching remission – indispensable in these days of heightened workloads – so that I could write some of this book. Thanks also to those who let me interview them about different forms of radical consumerism for various publications: Clive Barnett, Kalle Lasn, Juliet Schor and Kate Soper. And many thanks to everybody at *Soundings* meetings and gatherings for always making me think.

I'm hugely grateful to Steve Cross, Jeremy Gilbert, Sara Hackenberg and Liz Moor, who all read sections of the manuscript and gave me their advice. Their support has been enormously helpful. Even if, like a bad student, I didn't want to hear parts of their advice straight away, it always came back to me later and helped me sort out the thornier questions. Particular thanks to Sara Hackenberg for providing transatlantic galvanization when it was needed most, by reactivating Friday Club through the electronic ether; and to Jeremy Gilbert for gamely reading through the whole thing once it was finished. I'm grateful to Caroline Bressey, Nick Couldry, Kay Dickinson and Carol Tulloch for their apt reading suggestions and enjoyable conversations about writing.

Thanks to *Cultural Studies* for letting me reproduce Chapter 4, which originally appeared in Vol. 19 (2) of the journal in 2005; to Lawrence Grossberg and Mark Hayward for supporting the piece; and to Jonathan Rutherford and Lynda Dyson for helping me realize what needed sorting out. At the Open University Press, many thanks to Chris Cudmore, who backed the project from the beginning, Jack Fray, Melanie Havelock and the very helpful reviewers of the proposal.

Apart from that, thanks to all my friends, especially Roshi, Patty, Jus, Susanna, Liz, Mel, Lisa, Em, Paul, Adam, Hilary and Estelle for just being there when it was needed, to my extended families for all their types of support, and to Jeremy, for everything.

Introduction

The problems of contemporary consumerism have perhaps never been so conspicuous. It is, for instance, widely known that the sheer amount of products we consume, the energy they use and the rapid turnover of product life spans are connected to serious environmental damage and global warming – even if there is little agreement over what to do about it. The effects of the power of large corporations over small-scale producers, on the diversity of consumer choice and on local communities (whether through blocking access to cheap medicine, stunting the availability of different varieties of apple or aiding the generation of 'clone towns') have increasingly become the subject of anxiety. And social exploitation in the production of goods has become a heightened media issue: as the speed and availability of technologies increase, we can see and learn more about how those very technologies were produced using exploited labour, and about how clothing available on the high street was produced halfway around the world by children in sweatshops.

Problems with consumption are of course not new, and reactions to consumption's problems have some very long histories (Gabriel and Lang 1995; Cohen 2003; Hilton 2003, 2007). But in recent years these reactions have taken their own distinctively contemporary form and have led to a marked surge in 'alternative' consumer practices. Ethical consumption, fair trade, consumer protests, brand backlashes, green goods, boycotts and downshifting: these are all now familiar consumer activities – and in some cases, are almost mainstream. The specific constellation of anxieties about consumption has combined with the ever-expanding niche markets of neo-liberal consumer capitalism to generate an explosion in sales of 'ethical' goods. Fair trade consumption, for example, has boomed globally, with a 42 per cent increase in sales in 2006; in Switzerland, half the bananas bought are now fair trade (Nicholls and Opal 2005: 5; Fairtrade Foundation 2007). Recycling commodities and using less consumer goods (such as plastic bags) are more widely discussed issues than ever, providing key subject matter for newspaper and magazine articles, reality TV shows, films and documentaries (de Graaf *et al.* 2005; Barnett *et al.* 2007; Branston 2007; Parks 2007; Thomas 2008). Corporate brand-bashing has expanded from French farmers dismantling local branches of McDonald's and protests on the streets of Seattle through to mass-market books and films like *No Logo*, *Super Size Me* and *The Corporation* (Klein 2000; Bové and Dufour 2001; Abbot and Ackbar 2003;

Spurlock 2004). 'Green' products abound, with the expansion of specialist retail outlets and the mainstreaming of 'environmentally-friendly' goods in major retail outlets (Maniates 2002; Harrison *et al.* 2005; Williams 2007). And corporations are rushing to proclaim their 'ethical' credentials: to show us that they care, and that they are 'socially responsible' (Doane 2003a, 2003b, 2004; Kotler and Lee 2006; Henriques 2007).

This book suggests we might understand this phenomenon as an expanding field of 'radical consumption': for this is a world in which we are increasingly encouraged to shop for change. The book's primary aim is to put the 'radical' nature of these forms of consumption under interrogation, to question what is entailed by their appeal, and to ask: just how radical are they? To do so, it foregrounds a number of questions, including: is ethical consumption merely a sop for the middle classes? Can such forms of consumption ever move beyond their niche market status to become an effective political force? Should we understand corporate social responsibility as a form of consumer-oriented greenwash? And can we really buy our way to a better, more equitable or sustainable future?

Radical Consumption connects to a range of discussion and activity being mobilized around these subjects from its own specific role as an academic text. Consumer protest and ethical consumption have received much mainstream press attention in recent years, but academic discussion about it has until recently been noticeably limited. Emerging out of cultural studies and its adjacent areas, this book aims to expand the ways we have of discussing cultures that present themselves as 'ethical' or 'radical' alternatives to contemporary problems of consumerism. While emphasizing that there was never a 'Golden Age' of equal, non-commodified social relations to be nostalgic for, the book focuses on how radical consumption interacts with the complexities of the present: at a time when, as Arundhati Roy puts it, the key question is how to act in a world where there is no innocence and 'all our hands are dirty' (Roy 2004: 32). It argues that we need a more expansive vocabulary and to open up new approaches of enquiry in order to understand the area's many contradictions, strengths and weaknesses. To help create this, *Radical Consumption* makes links wherever possible to the embryonic new work which is gestating out of and across a number of disciplines (including geography, philosophy, sociology, film studies and politics) at the same time as putting to work a number of contemporary theories, terms and debates in media and cultural studies, including cosmopolitanism, reflexivity, cultural economies and ethics.

The book begins with a short theoretical chapter that considers how discourses of moralism and morality work to shape ethical consumption. Drawing on Wendy Brown's work, it suggests that ethical consumption can be understood as a 'crisis of moralism'; that it indicates both a kind of systemic paralysis of a wider system of consumption which is causing serious social, cultural and environmental inequalities and gestures towards the fact that on a wider scale significant alternatives to this system have not yet been forged to any significant degree. The chapter considers why it is that ethical consumption is today sometimes viewed as sanctimonious or pious. It locates this idea in relation to genealogies of morality and pleasure – in particular to what Colin Campbell called the 'romantic ethic' of modern consumerism – before looking at some of the ways in which such perspectives are being perpetuated and challenged today.

Chapter 2 broadens out the subject by discussing how in various ways we are often invited today to become what I term 'cosmopolitan caring consumers'. To explore this issue the chapter looks at three different case studies: American Express RED, Mecca Cola and Oxfam's Make Trade Fair campaign. These ventures all provide quite different ways of imagining modes of connection with other people around the globe through consumption: namely, through cause-related marketing, through an anti-American imperialism 'buycott' and through fair trade. The chapter draws on theories of cosmopolitanism to delineate the modes of global 'being' and 'caring' that we are encouraged to participate in through consumption, whether through charity, entrepreneurial solidarity or 'activist consumption'. By doing so, it confronts the question of how it is that some forms of 'caring consumption' have become more destructive than constructive.

Chapter 3 picks up on this subject by focusing on the development of corporate social responsibility: on how corporations have, over the past two decades in particular, increasingly attempted to show that they care about the broader society and the effects of their business. This chapter outlines the number of different perspectives that are taken on the subject of CSR, and shows how these positions do not, interestingly, map neatly onto a simple left/right political grid. Tracing the evolution of CSR in relation to earlier systems of corporate philanthropy and capitalist welfarism, it suggests that we can understand CSR as a post-Fordist promotional strategy which harnesses distinctive strands of these histories to try to compensate for new geographical distinctions and forms of inequality between contemporary producers and consumers. The question raised by this investigation of CSR is who should be responsible for responsibility: for CSR is in effect a struggle over the terrain over who can lay claim to the zone of responsible mature leadership.

Chapter 4 discusses how activists are taking on corporate attempts to expand their own power through consumer campaigns and actions. It addresses the issue of how contemporary consumer activists imagine their roles are and what they envisage as happening *after* the activist gesture. To do this it considers four different instances of consumer activism: the work of flamboyant dramatic activist Bill Talen, who, as Reverend Billy, stages mock-sermons in Disney and Starbucks stores; the stance of the late activist-entrepreneur Anita Roddick, founder of the Body Shop and author of the guide *Take it Personally*; the international network and magazine Adbusters, famous for its 'subvertisements'; and Naomi Klein's best-selling text *No Logo*. The chapter frames its discussion by looking at how 'reflexive' these different forms of contemporary consumer activism are, and in doing so explores the different meanings of 'reflexivity' in circulation in cultural theory, from the individualistic meaning of 'being present to oneself' to a more relational understanding of behaviour emerging out of a wider series of contexts.

Finally, Chapter 5 considers the possibilities and problems of green consumption by drawing on the 'ecosophy' of Félix Guattari. Broadly speaking, Guattari's theory emphasizes how different social, environmental and 'mental' systems or ecologies need to be thought together, and notes that discrepancies between or across these ecologies are damaging. Whilst considering some of the key areas of green consumption – recycling, green products and consuming less – this chapter uses Guattari's ideas to pick apart in detail the drawbacks that exist in the different ways they are practised and the potential for what they can become.

All the examples discussed in this book are stitched into larger stories; they are both indicative of wider trends, and distinctly particular. To only focus on their specificity, though, without attempting to 'think' them through wider dynamics, or to consider how they might connect to larger significances, would be to lapse into the stultifying zone that Bryan Turner calls 'complacent relativism' (Turner 2002: 45–64). As Ulrich Beck points out, this type of perpetual methodological micro-focus produces 'relativist essentialisms' (Beck 2006: 55) and breeds a tendency towards easy denunciations that bypass questions of how more kinds of global equalities are or might be able to emerge. Such complacent relativism is, Beck writes, blind to how interwoven histories, cultural intermingling and constant shifts are the historical norm, and to how any idea of non-intervention is an impossibility (Beck 2006). For we are always making 'interventions', however banal or significant, in one way or another, consciously or unconsciously: the interventions of the ordinary, the everyday, our being, talking, moving, doing and not-doing, collide to construct the world.

Radical consumption is one such area of intervention, and many claims are made for its radical or progressive nature by a wide range of different interest groups: from those who want to make more profit from selling commodities to those who hope to find in it solutions to some of the more apparently intractable problems of our time. The power being awarded to consumption is in part a reflection of the primacy given to the consumer in the 'post-Fordist' era since the 1970s in particular (Hall and Jacques 1989; Slater 1997), when attempts were made to 'roll back' the role of the state and increase the power of private and corporate enterprise. It would be more than naïve to think that any total or full-scale social redistribution of resources can be achieved solely through consumerism, given that most actions by consumers are made by precisely those segments of the global population with enough power to be able to buy. But equally consumer actions can be a very significant 'lever for change' (Barnett and Soper 2005) and it is important not to devalue the significance of consumption, as both cultural studies and the more recent academic industry of consumer culture studies illustrate (see, for example, Nava 1992, 1996 or Holt and Schor 2000). This is particularly the case given how, historically, the disparagement of consumption has been used to channel fears about the increased power of those groups newly 'enfranchised' into consumption: whether white women at the turn of the twentieth century 'knocking at the gates of power' (Huyssen 1987), emboldened teenagers from the 1950s (Hebdige 1981) or, more recently, shoppers in India and China. Responses to these forms of consumer discrimination have been complex. They have resulted both in facile celebrations of consumption which simply endorse a kind of corporate populism, or those more substantial accounts which are able to consider together both the gross inequalities of contemporary consumerism *and* the discriminations which have historically been made in consumption's name (see Winship 1980; Carter 1997; and McRobbie 2005, for good examples of the latter).

Equally, academic work can be very good at critiquing the problems of consumption while failing to recognize that there is always a need to generate what Raymond Williams once called 'resources of hope' (Williams 1989) or what, more recently, Laclau and Mouffe critique as 'the deficit of democratic politics to address the question of hope' (2003: 125). Radical consumption clearly can mobilize such an affect of hope, and this book argues that analysing it can, in modest and diversely situated ways, help us think through the extended cultural impact of our individual and collective actions as citizens and consumers. However, not all this change is progressive: as we will see, changes in consumption are clearly being used as levers for 'regression' as well as 'progression'. The challenge is neither to succumb to a corporate utopianism around the potential of radical consumption, nor a dystopian rejection that devalues its significance: but rather to recognize both its possibilities and limitations. That is why it is important to try to be wise to the complexities of these forms and discourses: so we can pick apart the elements that might seem to us to be useful and expansive, and those elements that seem to us to be retrograde and exploitative. This, in its various ways, is what this book tries to do.

1 Sanctimonious shopping?

Ethical consumption as a 'crisis of moralism'

'Ethical consumption' is a relatively modern term: established since the 1980s, it has gained popularity over the past decade in particular by gesturing towards a relatively broad discursive field, one which includes such diverse practices as buying fair trade, products-not-tested-on-animals, non-sweatshop brands, organic goods and avoiding 'exploitative' products or 'unnecessary' purchases (Gabriel and Lang 1995: 166–8; Crocker and Linden 1998; Micheletti 2003; Barnett *et al.* 2004, 2005, 2007; Micheletti *et al.* 2004; Harrison *et al.* 2005: 1). While the term has a relatively recent genealogy, as Matthew Hilton puts it, 'unloading a wider political baggage onto goods can hardly be described as a recent phenomenon and surely stretches as far back as one wishes to take a history of material culture' (2003: 313). Yiannis Gabriel and Tim Lang usefully schematize the modern incarnation of this longer history by splitting it into four main different stages, or 'waves': co-operative consumers; 'value for money' consumers, as represented by the magazine *Which?*; Naderism, after Ralph Nader's early legal work on the *Project for Corporate Responsibility* from the 1960s (which represented little Davids against the Goliaths of big corporations); and the 'alternative consumerism' that emerged out of the Reagan and Thatcher years, through which ethical consumption as we know it today became a powerful force (1995: 152–72).

As a term, 'ethical consumption' is often used rather flexibly, and tends to overlap and intersect with a variety of other phrases used to describe practices of consumer-driven social action. For historians such as Hilton, the most useful way of thinking about these collective practices is to consider 'consumerism' as 'a movement' (yet he notes that in its more recent stages, the history of this consumer movement is one in which *anti*-consumerism – meaning an opposition to consumer capitalism – has become increasingly prominent). Scandinavian social scientists such as Michele Micheletti have used the term 'political consumerism' since it emerged in mid-1990s Denmark at the time of the boycott of the oil company Shell (Micheletti 2003: x). And in the USA, the sociologist of consumer culture Juliet Schor favours the term 'conscious consumption' to emphasize the contemporary and historical purchasing practices of consumers who are 'mindful' of larger political and social contexts (Schor 2006). All these different terms have their different emphases and genealogies: for example, the Scandinavian term 'political consumerism' is loaded towards considering the actions of citizens through petitions and protests alongside the actions of consumers who buy; and 'consumerism' bears the hallmarks of the moment when the most significant phase of consumer protest in Europe was primarily directed towards having enough consumer goods at all, or about goods which were 'value for money', rather than the contemporary focus on sweatshops, animal welfare and global warming (Hilton 2003). 'Ethical consumption' is, however, perhaps the most common term used today in public discourse, and while its meaning is both relatively fluid and contested, its particular emphasis tends to be weighted, as we have seen, towards using purchasing power to sanction goods which have not been produced through exploitative conditions, however those conditions are defined. In this chapter, I want to consider the 'ethical' and 'moral' dimension of this discourse, in relation to its dominant positioning as a market-oriented consumer practice.

To begin with, it is useful to locate ethical consumption in relation to the larger context of novelty and fashion that is so fundamental to contemporary consumer culture. Colin Campbell influentially wrote that while production in modern capitalism was born out of the Protestant work ethic, with its elision of hard graft, delayed gratification and righteous virtue, it was the spirit of Romanticism, with its emphasis on novelty, individualism and desire which came to shape modern capitalism's *consumer* ethic (Campbell 1987). In other words, while Max Weber's account of the Protestant ethic could be used to 'explain' the formation of industrial modernity, through its story of the extension of a stern discourse of relatively joyless, hard-work-oriented Puritanism into new realms of social life, particularly production, and by emphasizing the pivotal role of this ethic as an engine of change, Weber's account, for Campbell, had far less to say about why people infused with such a joyless spirit of deferred gratification would ever come to be interested in the process of continually buying more and more stuff in the first, let alone second or third, place (Weber 1905/2003). It was instead the influence of a *Romantic* discourse, Campbell suggested, which could be used to understand the development of the consumer aspect of modern capitalism. It was Romanticism's drive towards novelty, passion and feelings and its valorization of individualism that was formative in the elaboration of a nascent fashion-system involving the rapid turnover of commodities. The implication of Campbell's thesis was, therefore, that it was this Romantic discourse or ethic that 'played a critical role in facilitating the Industrial Revolution and therefore the character of the modern economy' (1987: 2).

While Campbell's thesis has frequently been used to help explain the rise of modern consumer culture's rapid turnover of commodities through its appeal to individuality and self-fashioning (Bocock 1993; Lury 1996), the concept has rarely been used to discuss the practice of ethical consumption.

And if we do bring Campbell's thesis into dialogue with ethical consumption, a number of implications and lines of enquiry emerge. Perhaps the most obvious is how 'ethical consumers' use such forms of consumption to style the self: how ethical consumption is used, in post-Romantic consumer fashion, as a means of self-fashioning. While not necessarily conducted with reference to Campbell's work, this area is beginning to be perhaps one of the most readily explored lines of enquiry in recent studies on ethical consumption. For instance, Nelson *et al.* (2007) have discussed what kinds of civic participation and sociality freecyclers gain from joining the 'give and take' internet email list; Liz Moor and I have explored what image and idea of the self clothing company American Apparel offers its consumers through its aesthetic of 'transparency' (Littler and Moor 2008); and Parkins and Craig have analysed the forms of pleasure people gain from slow food (Parkins and Craig 2006: 86–118).

But in addition to the question of how consumers use ethical consumption as a means of self-fashioning, Campbell's analysis of the rise of the Romantic spirit of consumption working in counterbalance to a righteous and moral Protestant ethic of production also provokes questions about ethics and morality. One potentially interesting means of thinking about ethical consumption, for example, is to ask to what extent such practices act to *reverse* Campbell's paradigm. In other words, to what extent does ethical consumption work to *invert* the Romantic legacy of continual, sensual consumerism? To what extent do these contemporary practices of consumption mark a rebirth of its Puritan or Protestant inheritance? Indeed, to what extent might a spirit of quasi-religious moralizing and Puritanism perhaps become *reborn* in contemporary forms of ethical consumer practice?

In this chapter, I use Campbell's frame as a type of provocation in order to consider the place of morality and ethics in contemporary ethical consumption. For there is, as we are all probably very aware, a rich, charged, complicated and barely suppressed set of issues here around the question of sanctimoniousness and morality. To take but a few examples: who decides what is ethical about ethical consumption? Who gets to decide what is fair about fair trade? Don't a lot of these practices simply enable corporations to hold up their 'ethical' line as a niche market, while they continue to perpetuate exploitation through their regular range? Is ethical consumption merely a conscience-saving mechanism for the privileged? In turn, when does the critique of ethical consumerism become privileged liberal whining or navel-gazing? This chapter aims to drag such questions about morality, ethics and sanctimoniousness into the foreground.

In particular, what Campbell's theoretical framework provokes us into considering is how contemporary practices of ethical consumption might be situated in the context of longer-term genealogies. For it could be suggested that we might also situate ethical consumption in relation to this earlier moment that Campbell discusses by considering whether this formative conjunction between morality, Protestantism, Puritanism and Romanticism might have had some effect on contemporary forms of ethical consumption in particular as well as on consumption *per se*. In order to think about the discursive legacies of these issues, in this chapter I want to draw on the work of the contemporary American cultural and political theorist Wendy Brown on genealogies of moralism, pleasure, ethics and sanctimoniousness, as the schematizations she makes are helpful in opening up a means to think through some of these issues. In other words, I draw on Brown's work to consider how ethical consumption might connect both to the matrix of Romantic consumption that Campbell outlines and to its contestation, continuation and subversion through discourses of morality. To conclude, I consider how such patterns might play out in the present by looking at some specific examples.

Ethics: the new morality?

Wendy Brown's recent work on morality provides one interesting route into thinking about how contemporary practices of ethical consumption might be theorized in relation to the historical evolution of ideas of morality and sanctimoniousness (Brown 1995, 2001, 2005, 2006). This work is therefore worth outlining in a little detail as it will both help to set ideas about ethics and morality in a historical/theoretical context and to situate them in relation to the context of contemporary theoretical interests in academia. Brown's work, in a similar way to that of other philosophically-informed gender theorists like Elizabeth Grosz, has drawn on the nineteenth-century German philosopher Friedrich Nietzsche's ideas about morality to help make sense of contemporary habits and practices. Nietzsche's work, in particular in *Beyond Good and Evil* (1886/1994) and *The Genealogy of Morals* (1887/2003) asked, among other things, what was at stake in the meaning of morality. It questioned *who* was claiming the status of morality and *why*; and the uses of power which were being made in the name of, and through, it. Or, as Nietzsche put it: 'under what conditions did Man invent for himself those judgements of values, "Good" and "Evil"?' (Nietzsche 1887/2003).

In her book *States of Injury* (1995), Brown picked up some of these cues, in particular adapting Nietzsche's conceptualization of *ressentiment* to make sense of some of the sanctimonious dead ends that she thought critical and cultural theory was at that time finding itself in. The term *ressentiment* refers to the process through which a sense of resentment prompts action that is codified as just, and in which righteousness and inferiority act to ramify each other. This is a process Brown describes as 'the moralizing revenge of the powerless' leading to 'the triumph of the weak as weak' (Brown 1995: 67).

Brown, like Elizabeth Grosz, has used this concept to critique a liberal feminism which structures itself through perpetual dependency on its victim
status (and consequent reactive affirmation), which can simply work to
'reverse without subverting this blaming structure'. Grosz, for example,
describes the hole that certain types of liberal feminism digs for itself as a
'slave morality' which imposes a permanent and totalizing limit on women's
expression, because its emancipations 'must always remain reactive, ... tied to
oppression' (Grosz 1995: 15). (So, for instance, she uses this schema to argue
that certain feminist critiques to ban porn simply invert the problem rather
than disaggregating it, mirroring the straight male perspectives they mean to
critique.)[1] As Brown puts it, a more constructive way to jump is away from
ressentiment and into investigating the complexities of power plays, of the
struggles and wars of position around power, as a basis for opening up new
ways of thinking and acting, and of developing new ethical positions and
possibilities.

These readings of morality can themselves be situated as part of a wider
contemporary current in the humanities and social sciences which holds the
notion of 'morality' to be problematically loaded, saturated as it is with
connotations of a comfortably smug and relatively unreflexive stance. It is in
part such connotations that have led in recent years to the rising popularity of
the term 'ethics'. 'Ethics' is often now more frequently used and understood
as a word that has a similarity to 'morality' but is deemed to be more porous,
more open to be used in multiple ways, and which has more potential to carry
along with itself a greater degree of reflexivity as to how it is being used. The
popularity of 'ethics', in these terms, is a mark of the popularity of the virtue
ethics tradition of moral philosophy.[2] In relation to this tradition, Foucault's
use of the term has been influential, especially given that his particular usage
of the word 'ethics' always cleaved close to meaning a tool that could be used
to describe a style of behaviour or mode of conduct, or what he termed 'an
aesthetics of living', and was therefore always more open in the nature of its
use (Foucault 1983/2003: 200–6). At the same time, the expanding popularity
of the term is also due to interesting engagements with other branches of the
philosophy of ethics.

Through these multiple routes, 'ethics' in and around cultural studies
now comes with a wealth of connotations around openness and multiplicity
trailing behind it. In many quarters ethics has become the preferred term over
morality (see, for example, Zylinska 2005; Hawkins 2006) and, indeed, is
sometimes positioned as being completely *antithetical* to the term morality. In
either way it is perceived as helping to steer us away from the narrowly
programmable and towards the domain of contested meanings and reflexivity, and, in this sense, such intellectual activity in and around cultural
studies is also symptomatic of tendencies at large in wider realms of public
culture. Just imagine, for example, ethical consumption being called 'moral

consumption' – in a contemporary context, it sounds like a much more didactic term, po-faced, absolutist and antithetical to choice, which is why it isn't either a used or popular phrase. In this respect, the dominance of ethics over morality is mirrored in the wider context of Anglophone culture, or at least in its more libertarian and/or left-wing discursive strands.

'Ethics' is therefore used as a means of escaping dogmatic injunctions about obligation, to investigate custom and habit, or to open up new ways of thinking about mutual social responsibility, notions of the good and how actions might contribute to redressing gross imbalances of power. Its usage can be very particularly specified, or more casually slide between such meanings of custom and 'the good'. It therefore can often be useful to ask: what is being referred to when we talk about 'ethics'? What becomes imported into its meaning as it is popularized as a term, and what traces are sedimented within it? At times it can be worth questioning whether 'ethics' sometimes simply functions as a neologism, the new morality, smuggling some of its meanings in with it while it denies them in its insistence on its newness; or in the various returns to its earlier etymological meaning as 'custom' or 'habit' (an early meaning it shares, incidentally, with 'morality'[3]), whether there is any specificity to the word, or whether it becomes a relatively pointless term when we might as well use 'behaviour' or 'conduct'.

For Zygmunt Bauman, for instance, ethics and morality are deeply entangled, and the implicit apolitical relativism of many postmodern attitudes to ethics is profoundly problematic. Bauman suggests that we need to engage in 'returning moral responsibility from the finishing line (to which it was exiled) to the starting point (where it is at home) of the ethical process' (1993: 34). 'Greater morality', for Bauman, is what should be aimed for through the study of ethics, although this is not an easy process. Contemporary morality is always profoundly ambivalent, which is both its great strength and its greatest weakness: as he puts it, people in postmodernity are 'now forced to stand face-to-face with their moral autonomy, and also their moral responsibility. This is the cause of moral agony, this is also the chance that moral selves never confronted before' (Bauman 1995: 43).

From such a perspective, it becomes clear why for many the Nietzschean tradition that Wendy Brown's work is part of is problematic, both in its tendencies to throw out questions about how we can live together in a least exploitative fashion as possible (as Bauman and the virtue ethics tradition are able to discuss) with the bathwater of self-righteous versions of morality (and their attendant vested interests). This is particularly the case given that Nietzsche's writing does not readily lend itself to a sympathy for the exploited as well as the exploiters, which is another obvious problem for anyone who considers themselves to be even vaguely left-wing. After all, it is the 'slave morality' that Nietzsche finds most problematic and irritating, not the aristocratic kind. (A number of Nietzschean scholars have also pointed out the variety of internal contradictions within his attitudes to morality; see Ansell-Pearson 1994; Clark 1994; Foot 1994). However, Nietzsche's radical genealogy of 'morality' as a concept is profoundly useful in its effervescent and productive charge and its provocative opening-up of analysis. The insight that morality becomes annexed to ideas of the 'good' and 'the noble' through aristocratic practices clearly holds a lot of explanatory power for the way we might talk about the phenomena of patronage and charity today, both with and against the grain of Nietzschean analysis, as it were. In many ways the key problem is that, in effect, Nietzsche does not take the implications of his own insights far enough: he follows the routes of the tradition he critiques, re-fetishizing the notion of aristocratic morality and reinvesting 'the noble' in the aristocratic (because of its capacity to offer an energetic life-source) rather than disentangling their conceptual threads, as the work of some of his followers, like Brown, was later to do.[4]

Moralism and morality

Wendy Brown's later writing extends Nietzsche's interpretation of morality while simultaneously excavating its meanings in more sophisticated detail and adding a valuable genealogical dimension to the debate. In *Politics Out of History*, Brown makes a conceptual distinction between 'morality' and 'moralism', suggesting that there is a 'difference between a galvanizing moral vision and a reproachful moralizing sensibility' (Brown 2001: 22). This analysis partly comes from her exploration of the etymology of the terms. She notes that the *Oxford English Dictionary* defines 'morality' as 'ethical wisdom [or a] doctrine or system concerned with moral conduct or duty', but the definition of 'moralism' is quite different: it is 'an addiction to moralising ... [a] religion ... reduced to moral practice'. What she notices, in other words, that moralism seems to precisely *invert* the meaning of 'moral'; and this is partly because it comes afterwards, in its wake. So, as she puts it:

> From this account, moralism would appear to be a kind of temporal trace, a remnant of a discourse whose heritage and legitimacy it claims while in fact inverting that discourse's sense and sensibility. At the extreme, moralism may be seen as a kind of posture or pose taken up in the ruins of morality by its faithful adherents; it is thus a 'fall' from morality, a 'reversal' of morality, and an impoverished substitute for, or reaction from the evisceration of a sustaining moral vision.
>
> (Brown 2001: 23)

In these terms, 'moralism' can be understood as a kind of nihilism which poses as its opposite, 'morality'. Moralism is impoverished; it is *antithetical* to morality. Moralism becomes the place where *ressentiment* is located. In other words, Brown is using it to refine her reading of *ressentiment*, and also, interestingly, to critique Nietzsche's, by suggesting that he 'may have failed to distinguish adequately between active moral struggles against insubordination and the reproaches and nay-saying of what he called slave morality' (Brown 2001: 25–6). Her distinction between the bitter, morally bankrupt *ressentiment* of moralism and the more open possibilities of morality is illustrated for her through the example of Martin Luther King affirming the capacity of the subjugated to overcome: Brown describes his actions as an 'affirmative moral struggle' – a moral struggle with an *open* character that did not seek to fetishize a subjugated identity, but rather to engage in a temporally contingent and affirmative and collective project. In this respect, in emphasizing the tentative and social nature of affirmative moral struggles, she treads a similar, but much more specifically delineated, line to Bauman's provisional recuperation of the notion of morality in *Postmodern Ethics* and *Life in Fragments* (Bauman 1993, 1995).

While Brown fully acknowledges that morality can have a slightly uneasy relationship to power and interrogation – which, crucially, remain its consistent weak spots – it is also, equally crucially, marked by openness and affirming passion: it is positive and politically necessary. *Moralism*, on the other hand, shuts down debate, being 'intensely antagonistic toward a richly agonistic political or intellectual life'. Moralism shuts down what Chantal Mouffe calls agonistic debate, where all kinds of arguments can and *need* to clash with each other, rather than being driven underground (as is most graphically the case with mainstream 'Third Way' political debate) and which for Mouffe, like Brown (and indeed Nietzsche), is integral to any genuine space of democracy (Mouffe 2005).

This elaboration enables Brown to move beyond her previous work which reads the entire business of moral claims in the narrower terms of how they can be understood in relation to identity-as-injury. By refining the distinction between morality and moralism, and specifying the temporal implications of moralism being the resentful posture taken up when, for one reason or another, types of 'morality' haven't worked out, she is able to move into making what I think is a much more interesting larger interpretative gesture. This is to read 'moralism' as marking a crisis in political teleology. Moralism, in other words, marks '*a broken historical narrative to which we have not yet forged alternatives*' (my italics). As she puts it, moralism marks a crisis, is a stagnant phase (2005: 27). It 'lacks a vision of the future that overcomes the political significance of such differences, and thus lacks an affirmative collective project'. Moralism 'lacks what neo-Gramscians call a new hegemonic project', and in the process, it signifies a moment of political paralysis' (2005: 40).

Ethical consumption and the morality/moralism distinction

I would argue, Brown's definition of a distinction between a useful affirmative type of morality, which is both a necessary part of constructing any new political project (while it's something, it is nonetheless important to be careful of because of its capacity to slide into a cosy anti-intellectualism) and *moralism*, or its stagnant, worn-out trace, full of sanctimonious righteousness (a sentiment that's mainly there due to the fact that it's pretty much useless) holds some potential for understanding contemporary discourse on ethical consumption. 'Moralism' marks a crisis in political teleology, and is 'a broken historical narrative to which we have not yet forged alternatives'. The contemporary prominence of ethical consumption as a term, the very *incitement to discourse* around it, might, in a larger sense, we might say, mark a similar crisis in political teleology, a similar 'broken historical narrative to which we have not yet forged alternatives'. In other words, the very existence of a sphere of consumption that has to demarcate itself as 'ethical' does, on one important level, occupy similarly sanctimonious ground to Brown's space of 'moralism'. Or, to put it even more bluntly: ethical consumption should not need to be there; the wider system of consumption should be 'ethical'. The fact that this sphere *has to label itself as such* on some level represents a crisis in the imagined and practised political teleology of production and consumption.

Consumer pressure and activism have of course had a range of meanings, from campaigning for value for money and availability for all in post-war Europe, for example, to today's emphasis on green and non-sweatshop commodities (see Gabriel and Lang 1995; Hilton 2003, 2007; Nicholls and Opal 2005: 23). Moreover, as we have already noted, many of the problems 'ethical consumption' gestures towards today (particularly labour exploitation and environmental degradation) have been around, in various forms, for some time (Gabriel and Lang 1995; Hilton 2003, 2007). But the current popularity of 'ethical consumption' as a term and the specific character of its contemporary use indicates a particular kind, and exacerbated form, of 'crisis', propelled by global neoliberal consumer capitalism and ecological catastrophe. Its presence reveals both some of the key problems of our culture (global warming, global poverty, stark inequalities of wealth) and indicates the scale of our collective failure to deal with these problems on any significant or systemic level other than through small palliative measures orchestrated through the lifestyle choices of the sufficiently privileged. As Matthew Hilton puts it in his history of the consumer movement in the post-war West, the meaning of consumerism in contemporary culture has shrunk to mean expanded choice and services for the well protected and privileged of the North (2007: 80). We might say that the very existence of 'ethical consumption' as a category itself manifests the eruption of a righteous discourse of moralism because of this specific political impasse.

Moralisms/moralities in ethical consumption

But while this is a useful formulation in wider or 'macro' terms, it also remains a dangerous one if we use it in a totalizing way, or use it to reify an understanding of ethical consumption as fixed or immutable; for ethical consumption as a series of micropolitical practices and discourses is a diverse and complex area. What is true of the overarching phenomena is not, in other words, the end of the story, and the overarching phenomenon is a living one, mutable and shaped by a variety of discourses. We might therefore also ask: to what extent do *specific* instances or discourses around ethical consumption inhabit a realm of 'affirmative' and 'open' moral struggle as part of a collective project (or morality), and to what extent do they occupy a more defensive realm of static sanctimoniousness, or what Brown calls 'moralism'?

To explore these diverse threads, we might use a number of different approaches: for example, by analysing specific practices of ethical consumption and consumer protest and their practitioners' concepts of morality, ethics and action, which is a subject I return to later in the book (for example, in Chapter 3 on activism, and Chapter 5 on green consumption). But we might also take this chapter's concern with ethics, morality and consumer culture's romanticist/individualist roots a little further here by considering how their discursive inheritance lives on in contemporary cultural commentary. In this context, what Clive Barnett *et al.* have called the 'discursive construction' of ethical consumption becomes a useful tool. Making the important point that there is an 'irreducible dimension of mediation involved in working up of ethical consumerism as a field of action', Barnett *et al.* have noted that 'ethical consumption works through a set of subtle interpellations that turn upon ambivalent forms of address such as seduction and shame' (2004: 10).

The next section draws on such insights about the mediated nature of addressing ethical consumers to consider how ethical consumption is fashioned in relation to the shape and status of 'morality' in contemporary culture. It does this by gesturing towards, first, Colin Campbell's Romantic consumer matrix and, second, Wendy Brown's moralism/morality distinction are being perpetuated, challenged or negotiated in discourses around contemporary ethical consumption. For example, we might consider how ethical consumption 'passes through' the matrix of Romantic consumer culture; or how morality in ethical consumption is mocked; or how a rational non-Romantic ethical consumer subject is sometimes imagined or attempted to be willed into being. The aim of pulling out these strands is not merely to *describe* different forms of ethical consumption, but rather to attempt to open up some questions about how it is positioned in our culture – and in particular, how both 'morality' and the Romantic ethic of consumer capitalism function in relation to it.

Straw men? The 'worthiness' of ethical consumption

Ethical consumption, like any discursive formation, is diverse, and there are many different narratives in circulation around it. But one tendency is immediately noticeable when we start to look for evidence of morality/ moralism in ethical consumption practices. And that is that, to some extent, there is already a great *fear* of this phenomena in circulation, and that, in fact, it is also often actually quite difficult to find many actually existing examples of extreme moralism in ethical consumption discourse. Instead, this extreme moralism is more often than not posited as existing in the not-too-distant, recently imagined past. It often functions as a 'straw man'.

In other words, there is a common conception and anxiety that ethical consumption is, and particularly has been, in the immediate past, something that is overly serious in its aims, dour, not particularly interested in pleasure; in other words, puritan (or, to use a buzzword which has come into very frequent use during the past few years, 'worthy'). In becoming updated by passing through the zone of obligatory hedonism, or what Bourdieu described as 'a morality of pleasure as duty' in contemporary life (Bourdieu 1979/1986: 367), such practices can progress in the process to a more useful and pleasurable kind of morality.[5]

Many newspaper and magazine articles for example, begin with the sort of assumption expressed in the design magazine *Blueprint*:

> The next step is to bring much more imagination to the world of ethical products, to shift them from worthy to sexy. It will be a much brighter future when we're shopping for ethical products which we actually want, rather than those we feel we ought to want.
>
> (Livingston 2003)

This quotation can be connected to Colin Campbell's paradigm of modern consumerism as a phenomenon saturated with sensuality and hedonistic desire. Ethical consumption – at least before it accedes through this particular matrix – is positioned as being outside, as opposed to, this realm. In these terms, such a process of recuperation is happening partly because the very idea of ethical consumption can appear to challenge head-on consumer culture's Romantic ethic, its promise of plenitude, variety, choice and innovation. Ethical consumption is very easily available to be immediately positioned or ridiculed as involving reduced creative consumer choice – as overly 'worthy' and as sanctimonious.

In this way, the *imagined* or *actual* moralism of ethical consumption is therefore often positioned in the process of being 'updated'. It has to pass through the lens of Romantic, pleasurable consumption for it to be an acceptable contemporary identity. In other words, it's not a narrative or an identity that is deemed to be habitable until it can be updated by a new generation. In this sense it functions in a similar way to an imagined form of 'feminism' among young women (or 'Marxism' within certain strands of cultural studies). Angela McRobbie, for example, has recently described the process through which feminism is continually imagined as being, until the present moment, po-faced and moralistic. She discusses how this schema plays out a process of being rescued from

> the abject state to which feminism has been expelled (perhaps a retirement home in an unfashionable holiday resort) and from its status as that which is capable of instilling dread and horror in young women, for fear that they might be mistaken as a 'feminist'; and thus robbed of a sexual identity that counts and that has value.
>
> (McRobbie 2005: 189)

Ethical consumption can often become an entity which is imagined as occupying a recently unfashionable position; in this case, by occupying a place of puritan moralism. This process is conspicuously apparent in the case of companies such as American Apparel, the clothing company which explicitly brands itself around both an 'anti-sweatshop' message and the idea of being sexy, pleasurable and 'edgy' (Littler 2007; Littler and Moor 2008). Overtly sexualized images are a key part of its promotional message, and it is noteworthy that this discourse is frequently understood both by the company and commentary around it, as moving the brand away from 'worthiness'. In the words of one article, 'the fact that the ads really do look like out-takes from homemade porn stops American Apparel seeming too worthy' (Collard 2005). It is the taken-for-granted nature of this opposition that is interesting – or in other words, why exactly is it that being 'worthy' is never 'sexy'? – and it is an opposition that can be understood by returning to Colin Campbell's schema. For the answer is that being worthy is part of a string of associations (what Laclau and Mouffe would call 'a chain of equivalence'), which interconnects the Protestant work ethic with Puritanism, with hard work, and with a religious-derived moralism. It is the *other* side of the equation – sexualization, pleasure and consumption – which disturbs such connotations.

There are various arguments as to why this process, of ethical consumption passing 'through' what we might call the 'Romantic consumption matrix', might be a good or a bad thing. Its passage through this system is problematic namely in that it has to pass through a consumer fashion-system valorizing the endless production of more and more goods, which in purely quantitative terms (i.e. of energy consumption) hardly contributes to the lessening of global warming. And this endless system of production is of course articulated to the structural inequalities of late capitalism. On the other hand, there are good arguments as to why passing through this matrix is less problematic, or even necessary: for it would be pointless and arrogant for any type of ethical consumption to ignore the complexities, multiplicities and constant production of desire and identity (see Hawkins 2006). One route out of this apparent impasse, or one obvious imagined 'ideal' for ethical consumer products, then, would be a process which both enabled or engaged with the complexities of desire and identity *and* produced goods under relatively equal economic conditions *and* reduced energy consumption.

But there are other implications of the positioning of ethical consumption as a state that can be ridiculed as outdated, worthy and in need of 'updating'. As McRobbie points out, consigning categories like feminism to a sad and abject state from which they today need 'rescuing' involves an act of distancing oneself from the broader political power, impact and challenge which such movements have historically had before selectively connecting to some of its strands as an individual (or to put this formulation in one of its more familiar terms: 'I'm not a feminist, but …'). The discourse in which ethical consumption is ridiculed as an abject series of practices which one needs to distance oneself from before it can be associated with as a 'modern and sexy' practice has some similarly disturbing connotations. It works by implicitly ridiculing the broader history of political consumer action as 'worthy', and by marginalizing and neutralizing the broader forms of collective action and political history that ethical consumption is part of. In this way, the imagined moralism of ethical consumption can work to 'check' the practice of ethical consumption before it spirals into a fuller critique of consumer capitalism: it positions ethical consumption as an acceptable discourse when it is made 'sexy' through the individualistic channels of new forms of commerce. As with McRobbie's analysis of the selective 'rescuing' of feminism which negates its historical power and collectivity, this discourse around ethical consumption often mobilizes a fear of 'political correctness' to neutralize its connection to a broader, collective and political movement in the process.

Moral instruction

Perhaps the closest to the oft-imagined position of 'moralism' exists in the form of populist exhortations and how-to guides on shopping ethically.

These provide various kinds of moral and ethical instruction that vary in tone and format but usually seek to rationally guide behaviour. The guidebook *Save Cash and Save the Planet*, published by Collins and Friends of the Earth, for example, opens by telling the reader that

> By flipping through this book you will find clear answers to help you reduce your negative impact on people and the planet, save money and make you feel good. On the way you will find real-life stories to help inspire you to make positive life changes.
>
> (Smith and Baird 2005: 14)

The mixture of information and inspiration to rationally shape individual consumer behaviour is a common motif. It could be argued that such books place too much emphasis on the power of the consumer to engineer social change; that they replicate, in inverted fashion, the ideology of the sovereign consumer of free market economics. Such an argument has been the subject of a fair amount of discussion in political science and sociology, with Michelle Micheletti, for example, challenging this view by arguing that such ethical consumption needs to be understood as 'individualised collective action', as prompted by individual citizens, yet transmuting into larger collective patterns of behaviour (see Micheletti 2003). Micheletti tends to be overwhelmingly and almost uniformly optimistic about the effects of such action, rather than seeing any significant problems with the logic of such atomized post-Fordist politics. Similarly, but in less gung-ho fashion, Clive Barnett *et al.* have discussed how information sources such as *The Good Shopping Guide* and the *Ethical Consumer* magazine published in the UK by ECRA (the Ethical Consumer Research Association) consist of a form of action which

> [i]s not solely focussed on simply changing individual consumer behaviour. It is, rather, indicative of a type of 'politics of shame' in which one set of collective actors (campaigns, NGOs, charities) engage with other collective actors (retailers, suppliers, corporations) through the real and discursive figure of 'the ethical consumer'.
>
> (Barnett *et al.* 2007)

'Shaming' such collective actors into action might be read, to use Wendy Brown's terms, as a means by which a potential moralism (bitter inactive sanctimoniousness) becomes used and converted into a more open, collaborative and active form of morality, in which it is used strategically to attempt to effect active change. In this way, moralism/morality is mobilized as a lever, rather than an end, unto itself.

Mocking moralism

This brings us to the issue of how it is often more common, now, for ethical consumption in some way to take part in the *mocking* of moralism, whether this takes a subtle or extreme form. For example, a recent advert promoting the British retail store Marks and Spencer's (M&S) new line of fair trade clothing gently mocks its own complicity in a holy moral discourse by using the tagline 'Bless our fairtrade cotton socks'. The advert mobilizes a quasi-religious narrative of enlightened self-interest: it will make both you and your conscience comfortable. It also indicates something of the historically strong connections between fair trade consumption and faith groups, and the wide variety of articulations that have been made from this point, from socialist forms of Christianity to patronizing missionary discourses of healing (Barnett *et al.* 2006). But clearly the M&S ad is teasing its own position as a company advertising its own moral standards.

This construction of a light-hearted morality is interesting in the light of the company's history, as it is itself indicative of some of the larger shifting social meanings of ethical consumption in 'the West' or 'the North'. Paradigmatic of Fordist paternalism, M&S dramatically turned around its shoddy reputation for paying poor wages in the 1930s to come to have 'the highest reputation as an employer by the 1970s' for both its retail and production staff (Bevan 2001: 34). This was a key factor in its achieved stature as certainly a trusted, and to a large extent, a perceived *'ethical'* retail institution. More recently, M&S has moved from a company concerned with the ethics of production in terms bound up with *national* labour – as a company with a strong reputation for producing goods in British factories and paying 'reasonable' wages – to an organization which in the 1990s joined the bulk of other large chain stores to outsource production overseas and to use cheap labour in the global economy.

We might say that Marks and Spencer appears to be attempting to recoup some of the 'ethical' dimension of its brand image that was lost in the 1990s, and bestow upon itself a certain niche distinction through its promotion of a fair trade line of clothing. Interestingly, the paternal nationalism with which the M&S brand identity has for so long been bound up is able to be re-articulated here on a more international basis through its connection to the paternalism/maternalism offered by fair trade (see Zick Varul 2008). Its morality, in other words, is mobile, and it is saturated with irony. The appeal of such mocking moralism can be explained by how, as Bauman puts it, 'moral life is a life of continuous uncertainty. It is built on the bricks of doubt and cemented with bouts of self-depreciation' (1995: 3).

What is notable in such cases is that the status and the position of morality and ethics are being questioned. Such questioning moralities are moralities which are fluid, liquid, malleable. And at the same time, the status of what is *too* moralistic, and what can *reasonably* be done, is worried away at: the imagined position, the straw position of overt moralism has been a movable position. When public anxieties ratchet up further about global warming, for example, the location of 'overt' moralism can allow other, safer, productive moralities to be inhabited near it, by contrast, shifting the goal-posts of its relative identity.

But equally this should not blind us to how 'morals' do not necessarily have to be used to reinforce or promote ethical consumption. A significant way moralism can be deployed, for example, is not only through sanctimonious greens, but through downright hostility to ethical consumption: for example, in Britain, a self-righteous voice like that of popular TV personality and ethical consumption sceptic Jeremy Clarkson is often heard resisting any movement towards green consumption, on the libertarian grounds of not wanting to be told what to do. So while moralities are mobile, moralism can also become locked into entrenching a variety of destructive positions.

Conclusion: mobile moralities

This chapter has suggested that Campbell's influential formulation might be used to consider ethical consumption: to ask, to what extent is contemporary ethical consumption similarly hedonistic and individualistic, and to what extent does it subvert such a paradigm, re-importing notions of Puritan simplicity? To consider this question, it drew on the work of Wendy Brown, and particularly the genealogical and methodological distinction she notes between morality and moralism: moralism is an exhausted political narrative, righteously sanctimonious, impotent and the place of *ressentiment*; morality is a more ambivalent concept, one which has the possibility for sanctimoniousness but simultaneously also functions as a place holding the necessary potential for social and cultural change.

The contemporary prominence and the incitement to discourse around ethical consumption, the chapter argued, mark a similar crisis in political teleology to Brown's 'broken historical narrative to which we have not yet forged alternatives'. Ethical consumption as a category which is over-whelmingly oriented to meaning a segment of consumer culture manifests the eruption of a righteous discourse of moralism propelled by our contemporary neoliberal conjuncture. At the same time, the field of ethical consumption is not static or fixed, but complex. It exhibits strands of both moralism and morality.

Wendy Brown's work therefore enables us to think more capaciously about how ethical consumption might both connect to the matrix of Romantic consumption that Colin Campbell outlines and to its continuation, contestation and subversion in contemporary discourse. The common motifs in circulation that I looked at in the last section illustrate these connections. I argued that the idea of ethical consumption as 'worthy' rather than 'sexy' was to raise anxieties about its position as a kind of moralism, but can also be understood through Colin Campbell's schema of the Romantic ethic of modern consumerism, in that it disturbs long-standing historical connections between the ideas of consumerism, individualism and novelty. Because of these genealogies, the moralism of ethical consumption is now more routinely taken as a phenomenon to be mocked, even by those who participate in its domain. This indicates how ethical standards are actively being *repositioned*, or the 'mobility of moralities' around ethical consumption – a phenomenon that can be read in relation to both the concept of 'consumer choice' and to the mobility of meaning itself which makes cultural change possible.

One notable discourse, I argued, is that in which 'worthy' ethical consumption is often positioned as a straw man, a stage that needs to be worked past by a more 'sexy' stage of contemporary consumer culture. This is a formulation that can again be understood in relation to Romantic individualist consumerism, particularly when connected to Bourdieu's idea of obligatory hedonism, or pleasure as duty. But we can also see in such narratives the drive to neutralize the perceived 'threat' of a political movement by positioning a broader series of political and historical contexts that ethical consumption can clearly be contextualized in relation to as outdated and abject. The disavowal of the importance of the forms of collective politics that ethical consumption can, in one important way, be linked with, and its selective rechannelling as 'sexy' only when completely divorced from these connections and channelled through new commercial opportunities, is a discourse which works to foreclose the strands of radical potential it might have.

Contemporary ethical consumption discourses, then, can contain elements of reproach and sanctimoniousness. They can exhibit affirmative drives, imagination, and a vitalizing energy in building alliances or networks. 'Morality' can be mobilized in a variety of ways to contribute towards the governance, invention in or self-fashioning of consumer behaviour. It can also – as we will see in subsequent chapters – be understood in terms of what mixture of discourses it advocates: consuming less, a pro- or anti-capitalist stance, participation in ideas of decluttering the self and the shape of its moral positioning. So while we might say that the overall *existence* of the formation signifies moralism, or a crisis in political teleology, looking at the complexities and differentials in this area means that we can find possibilities and potential as well as paralysis and reproach. But there are many questions which the framework I have pursued in this chapter does not, and cannot ask; and some of these are what the following chapters pursue.

2 Cosmopolitan caring

Globalization, charity and the activist-consumer

> RED works by embodying the idea that what we collectively choose to buy, or not to buy, can change the course of life and history on this planet. 'It's so smart,' Gisele explains. 'You're going to do it anyway, you're going to go shopping. But now you can buy something and help someone else at the same time. [RED] is bold, it's strong, it's powerful.'
>
> (Alexandra Heminsley, 'When Gisele Met Keseme',
> American Express RED website)

It is 2006. The American Express RED card is being launched. Its glossy promotional campaign features Giselle Bündchen, the German-Brazilian super-model – beloved by the celebrity-spotting press for her looks, salary, and status as the ex-girlfriend of Leonardo DiCaprio – alongside two Kenyan Masai warriors. The RED card, the campaign blurb tells us, will divert 1 per cent from each shopping purchase to The Global Fund 'to help fight AIDS in Africa'. Conceived by U2 pop star Bono and businessman Bobby Shriver to 'get big business excited about the fight against AIDS', Product RED was launched with a number of partners, mainly high-end fashion brands and iconic global corporations. American Express was one of the first few companies to get on board a range of RED products which, alongside the American Express card, includes RED iPods, RED Gap shirts and RED Motorola phones. The website describes these activities as a way to 'buy something and help someone else at the same time'; as a way, through shopping, to 'change the course of life and history on this planet'.[1]

The RED campaign is just one of the many ways today in which we are presented with the possibility of being both cosmopolitan and caring through consumption (or with what we might call, to put it more pithily, 'cosmopolitan caring consumption'). Cosmopolitan literally means 'citizen of the world', and a variety of organizations and corporations sell us the idea that through buying their product, we can make the world a better, fairer, healthier, more just, more habitable or more equal place. But they also prompt a large and important question. To what extent do they merely paper over the cracks of global social injustice – or even deepen them more fully – and to what extent do they offer possibilities for 'progressive' change?

This chapter aims to provide some potential lines of enquiry to help open up this question. It suggests that we might look at some of the different forms such globally-minded caring consumption takes; and that we might draw on the recent interest in theories of cosmopolitanism to do so. The term 'cosmopolitanism', derived from the Greek words for 'world' and 'citizen', was a phrase developed by the Greek Stoic philosophers, one reworked in the eighteenth century by Kant to evoke an idea of a global community and to gesture, with Enlightenment optimism, towards how it might be possible to imagine oneself as a citizen of the world (Beck 2006). Recently – particularly over the past decade – 'cosmopolitanism' has been revisited as an idea in the humanities and social sciences as a way to think about how global forms of connection, sociality and belonging might function in a contemporary context. It has become the focus of interest because it appears to offer a way of conceptualizing both our relationship to a broader global community and how we 'live with difference at home'. As a term, then, it offers an additional and different focus from that of the perpetually exploitative dynamics of 'imperialism' or 'colonialism', and from a different angle to the existing set of debates implied by the term 'globalisation' (with its recurring emphasis on cumulative process). Cosmopolitanism is therefore in part attractive because it offers what Raymond Williams once termed 'resources of hope' (Williams 1989): because it appears to open up a different kind of imaginative space by gesturing towards ways of thinking about how we might be able to have a positive and dynamic relationship to other people in the world alongside accounting for the exploitations which exist.

At the same time, contemporary debates on cosmopolitanism have shifted since their earlier incarnations. Much of the contemporary debate circulating around the term has focused on to what degree 'cosmopolitanism' valorizes a form of mobility or an epistemological position primarily available to the ultra-privileged, as embodied by those with enough money to travel at will or consume cheap labour 'at home' (Morley 2000: 225–45).[2] But being cosmopolitan, as Mike Featherstone points out, is not necessarily the exclusive position of the privileged; the asylum seeker is also 'cosmopolitan' (Featherstone 2002: 1–15). Nor is cosmopolitanism necessarily politically right-on or emancipatory: the cosmopolitan citizen, as James Clifford puts it, for example, might be the 'business migrant riding the crest of capital flows unrestrained by citizenship', rather than the alter-globalization protestor (Clifford, quoted in Cheah and Robbins 1998: 21; Featherstone 2002).

The genealogies of the term are also being more extensively discussed today in order to debate in what kind of cosmopolitan present we are (or are not). For example, Ulrich Beck suggests that we are in a fourth stage and that there have been at least 'three historical moments' of cosmopolitanism before the present; the first being the Greek Stoics who laid the foundation of the idea, the second being optimistic Kantian universalism, and the third being Hannah Arendt and Karl Jaspers' confrontation with the issues of war, violence and the 'breakdown of civilisation' (Beck 2006: 45–6). Timothy Brennan locates the negative connotations of the subject a little earlier in the twentieth century than Beck by discussing Georg Simmel's interest in cosmopolitanism as both cause and symptom of the quasi-colonial expansion of urban centres (Brennan 2003: 43).[3] And Jacques Derrida strips the theory inside out, excavating its Eurocentricism but arguing that we should use its insights to move beyond a tired, and disabling, Eurocentric/anti-Eurocentric binary; to conceive of a 'cosmopolitanism to come' which would pose the question of how, globally, we might offer forms of 'unconditional hospitality' (Derrida 2001).

In such a variety of forms, contemporary debates on cosmopolitanism are therefore now invariably keen to emphasize the *multiplicity* of possible cosmopolitanisms, the *variability* of power relations they entail, and in doing so to dissociate themselves from Kant's Enlightenment dream of a singular cosmopolitan stance progressing towards a singular worldwide community (Cheah and Robbins 1998; Featherstone 2002: 2). There has been a shift towards emphasizing what is variously termed 'critical cosmopolitanism' (Rabinow 1996, quoted in Beck 2002) or 'discrepant cosmopolitanisms' (Clifford 1998) or 'cosmopolitics' (Cheah and Robbins 1998; Derrida 2001). As Pheng Cheah and Bruce Robbins outline, for example, discussing their use of the latter term:

> The neologism cosmopolitics is [...] intended to underline the need to introduce intellectual order and accountability into this newly dynamic space of gushingly unrestrained sentiments, pieties, and urgencies for which no adequately discriminating lexicon has had time to develop.
>
> (1998: 9)

In other words, there is both an awareness of the diversity of forms of power relations involved in 'being cosmopolitan' and the forms of 'world openness' (Featherstone 2002: 13) this might involve, and an attempt to expand the range of expression through which such forms can be explored and understood. This necessarily means asking hard questions of the well intentioned; for, as Beck puts it, 'only a devil's advocate who questions well-meaning cosmopolitanism as to its emancipatory function and its misuse can open the debate over the ethics and politics of cosmopolitanism' (2006: 47). We might note here that, in this sense, the term has travelled similarly to the debates circulating around the term 'hybridity', which has increasingly since the 1990s moved beyond celebrating combinations of difference, and the breadth and historical range of cultural fusion, to an emphasis on the varied power relations, both nice and nasty, constituting such hybridities (see Brah and Coombes 2000). In these terms, a critical sense of cosmopolitanism or cosmopolitics can potentially be used as a way to open up and generate further thought about how the complex and multiple ways in which we are citizens of the world – or not permitted to be citizens of the world – might be understood.

It is therefore, I am suggesting, worthwhile bringing some of these cosmopolitan theories and concerns to bear on a realm of consumption in which buying is presented as a means to intervene in issues of global injustice. For while, as Roberta Sassatelli puts it, 'it would be mistaken to simply suppose that the "consumer" now realizes a new "global citizenship"', it has come to be widely acknowledged that there are an increasing number of ways in which consumption and consumer actions have become more clearly connected to 'issues of global equality' (Sassatelli 2007: 226). In this chapter, I explore this subject by focusing on a few recent high profile case studies: American Express RED, Mecca Cola and Oxfam's 'Make Trade Fair' campaign. The examples are chosen because they offer quite different perspectives on what 'a caring cosmopolitan consumer' might involve, or look like. Broadly speaking, they fall into three different categories: the American Express RED campaign offers a type of cosmopolitan charity consumption through cause-related marketing; Oxfam, a variety of activist/fair trade consumption aimed at changing global trade rules; and Mecca Cola, a form of pro-Islamic anti-US-imperialist consumption.

This chapter therefore examines something of the *range* of claims that are being made about how we, as caring consumers, can be part of a global community, and indicates something of the complexities of these areas. It does so by interrogating the types of cosmopolitanism they produce, by analysing the discourses they create, the types of cultural economy they participate in, and the imagery they project. I am not claiming that these are the only categories, or models, of caring cosmopolitan consumption that exist, nor that there are not overlaps between them, nor that these particular examples can be taken as somehow being completely representative. Rather, I am rather suggesting that these are indicative of tendencies which have a certain cultural currency and ascendant power, and that because of this they are worth paying attention to. To begin with, let's return to the American Express RED card.

Seeing RED: cause-related marketing and cosmopolitan capitalism

> Cosmopolitanism is no longer a dream but has become a social reality, however distorted, which has to be explored.
>
> (Beck 2006: 46)

The American Express RED credit card is a form of charity consumption, or, more specifically, 'purchase-triggered donation' which acts by diverting 1 per cent from each shopping purchase to The Global Fund 'to help fight AIDS in Africa'. One of the campaign's key images depicts supermodel Giselle and Kenyan Masai warrior Kesame laughing and playing around together on a photo shoot. She is in a deep scarlet *haute couture* dress, curly hair blowing casually, gown split open at the thigh to reveal a long, tanned leg. He is in full Masai costume, standing on one leg, his arm around her shoulder. The image is casual, yet precisely posed. It is a performance of relaxed, glamorous fun, and of intimacy between sharply choreographed and highly visible cultural difference. The accompanying narrative describes the joyful 'rapport' that emerged between the two over the duration of the photoshoot. Apparently their connection, as manifest in this picture, as

> not just a fabulous representation of American Express RED's passion for positivity, but also an expression of the joy that bringing two such different worlds together can so tangibly create. It turns out you can change the world while keeping a smile on your face.[4]

The imagery of the American Express RED campaign is of an affluent kind of cosmopolitan hybridity. Giselle Bündchen's stylized appearance is used to emphasize a casual, 'effortless' experience of fun, high-end glamour. This glamour is echoed through the text's description of how RED cardholders can 'feel great about spending, whether you're buying cappuccinos or cashmere', because of the combination of altruism combined with 'Exclusive RED deals on boutique hotels, hip restaurants and other life-enhancing treats'.[5] The website highlights its connections with the other high-end brands involved in the RED campaign, such as fashion designer Georgio Armani, further underlining how its interpellated consumer is glamorous, affluent and hedonistic.

This is the type of cosmopolitanism which Bruce Robbins describes as belonging to the tradition of the right, which builds its 'association of cosmopolitan globality with privilege', and is organized around motifs such as 'classy consumption, glossy cleavage, CNN, modems, faxes, Club Med, and the Trilateral Commission' (Robbins 1998: 248). As the work of Mary Louise

Pratt and Huang Teo make clear, such a discourse has a long history, and can be traced through the cosmopolitan figure of the aristocratic traveller in particular (Pratt 1992; Teo 2002). It is worth noting that this combination of glamour and altruism offered by RED is channelled not only through the buying of objects, but *experience*. By offering 'the chance to win REDpass competitions which unlock fabulous experiences which money simply cannot buy'; alongside experiencing the feeling of altruism through the 1 per cent donations, RED gives its consumer the possibility of further incursions into what Pine and Gilmour (1999) have termed 'the experience economy'.

At the same time, the discourse of cosmopolitanism-as-privilege is combined here with two others: with that of cosmopolitanism-as-international community and cosmopolitanism-as-imperial-benevolence. The benevolent dynamic in which the Western consumer is being invited to 'help' Africa through donations has its roots in the history of colonialism and empire, and there are in the American Express RED campaign pronounced echoes of the missionary ethos of nineteenth-century European imperialism, when the idea that Africans needed to be helped to pull themselves out of primitive infantilism by the 'mother countries' was used to justify a system which kept the Europeans in power so they could draw on Africa's natural resources and wealth (Hall 1998: 190–1). Clearly the positioning of Keseme in full Masai warrior garb next to the high-fashion whiteness of Gisele also needs to be located in the tradition of constructing images of stark cultural difference and exoticized otherness (Hall 1992). This image is a graphic illustration of the truism that, in contemporary capitalism, 'cultural difference sells': of cultural difference being used by privileged (and overwhelming white) Western consumers as a kind of 'exotic spice' to liven up their lives (see hooks 1992). While the use of a charitable iconography of difference has a very long history (see Ramamurthy 2003), the distinct 'take' here is that it is combined with a discourse of cosmopolitanism-as-privilege. American Express RED offers luxury consumption combined with exoticized difference, and topped off with an affective glow of charitable imperialist endeavour.

It is equally significant, in the context of how traditional imperialist dynamics are being reworked and reproduced, that charity is being reconfigured as a kind of equitable and *fun* relationship between an international community of people. Here 'the West and the rest' are presented as embracing on 'equal' terms: they are arm in arm. The commentary quotes Gisele saying 'This picture is real. We loosened up and we were hanging out and laughing, and that's when it worked' (Heminsley 2007). Both this 'equal' relationship, and the very *effort* that has to go into producing it, are highlighted. While it features a German-Brazilian supermodel representing 'the West', this undeniably still works to promote a light-skinned version of female sexual attractiveness. RED is trying to make caring cosmopolitan consumption sexy: to make it sexually charged with the glamour of a high-end fashion magazine.

While such sexualization marks a shift away from the *puritan* nature of such imperialist, missionary-oriented traditions, it does not mean these cultural dynamics necessarily become less imperialistic, but simply less puritan. It's only still too obviously bound into some very traditional terms – clearly Gisele's Western femininity empowered through glamour has most control. In terms of cultural representation, the RED campaign therefore performs, culturally, a kind of cosmopolitanism-as-privilege which attempts to *in part* move away from an image of imperial benevolence by gesturing towards a shared global community; but which does not bypass it and instead continues to partially perpetuate its discourse of imperial benevolence.

But while it is important, it has also now become fairly easy to point out imperialist imagery; and such approaches can have a tendency to bypass the question of how change can happen. More challenging questions to ask today might be: are such dynamics of 'imperialist benevolence' an inevitable part of any attempt to redistribute resources? And: how do such new techniques and developments in cosmopolitan charitable consumption connect to issues of exploitation and redistribution at other levels besides – and in conjunction with – the imagistic?

To understand this dynamic in more detail it is helpful to explore the 'cultural economy' of such cosmopolitanism (see du Gay 1997; du Gay and Pryke 2002) and to look more closely at how this mode of charity consumption operates. The yoking together of charity and consumption is not new. We might think, for example, of the promotional badges that people buy to show their support, or second-hand shopping in charity shops. But today, as befits the ever-burgeoning array of niche markets of post-Fordist consumer capitalism (Wernick 1991; Hall 1997; Slater 1997), this range of charity consumption has widened. Charities offer a number of ways of 'buying into' their message beyond that of simply donating money, as the slew of marketing publications on the subject graphically attests (see for instance Sargeant 2004; Bruce 2005; Quelch and Laider-Kylander 2005; Kotler and Andreasen 2007). Established charities like Oxfam have expanded their range of shopping outlets and formats to include high-end 'quality' boutiques, and 'trendy' customized clothing emporiums like TRAID, established in 1999, have emerged (Gregson and Crewe 2003: 40–9). Rubber charity wristbands provide a youthful variant on the older practice of buying pins and badges. And we can also buy 'charity' variants of 'regular' products – a form of charity brand extension – including credit cards and mobile phones like those supplied by product RED.

In this respect, one crucial aspect of the RED campaign is its specific form of what has become known as 'cause-related marketing' (CRM): a strategy in which corporate brand identities and products are connected to charity or non-profit organizations, primarily through the sale of commercial products with a percentage of the profits being channelled to the 'good cause' in question (Theaker 2002: 209–17). Other high-profile examples of CRM include the pink products sold by a range of companies in alliance with breast cancer charities – from cosmetics giant Estée Lauder through supermarket retailer Wal-Mart to the luxury crystal company Swarovski – during Breast Cancer Awareness Month in October. Since it emerged in the early 1990s CRM has expanded enormously to the extent that in the USA corporations have spent over a billion dollars on it. Culturally, CRM works through a consumer strategy that allows cosmopolitan caring to be linked to consumer hedonism: in other words, not by focusing on denial or abstention, but as a simple 'choice' which can be made by consumers to assist 'effective positive change'. As Bono says of product RED, for example:

> Philanthropy is like hippy music, holding hands. Red is more like punk rock, hip-hop; this should feel like hard commerce [...] I'm calling it conscious commerce for people who are awake, people who think about their spending power and say, 'I've got two pairs of jeans I can buy. One I know is made in Africa and is going to make a difference and the other isn't. What am I going to buy?'
>
> (Milmo 2006)

Through such rhetoric CRM appears profoundly uncontroversial. Everybody appears to be helped: consumers get to contribute without significantly changing their behaviour, while brand value is added to the corporation; or as journalist Sarfraz Manzoor (2006) outlines in an article featured on the RED website:

> When people are told that something is for a good cause they are more likely to get involved; the promise that their spending will help others means more of us are willing to splash out on phones and use our credit cards. Meanwhile the brands themselves are refreshed and given the sheen of the cutting edge and their bosses get to hang out with Bono. One woman referred to it as punk capitalism, but in fact it is more cappuccino capitalism; it accepts that most of us want nice things and rather than berating us, it suggests that there might be ways in which our consumerism could help others. The cleverist aspect to the [RED] campaign is how it doesn't try and persuade consumers to change their behaviour and it doesn't play to their guilt; instead it appeal to what are known as 'midpath realists'.

In these terms, CRM is presented as a system in which everybody 'lucks out'. CRM appeals to corporations because they can create a positive image for their brand and create emotional ties with consumers based on cosmopolitan caring and integrity. Maximum 'goodness' plus extra sales and consumer happiness are therefore achieved with the minimum of fuss through the simple tactic of synergy. CRM appears to be a 'win–win' situation. What could there possibly be to complain about?

However, as Inger Stole has discussed, 'what might seem like a fair exchange between corporations in search of goodwill and non-profits in search of funds also raises a range of troubling social, political and ethical questions'. First, causes are selected in terms of how they will provide added value to the brand, which means that non-profit causes which do not appeal to the corporation's target market will 'are ignored, even if they do vital work, while groups that provide good marketing vehicles receive a disproportional amount of interest'. For example, in CRM's early days in the early 1990s, AIDs-related charities were completely ignored, because the link to homo-sexuality frightened their target market. CRM's cleavage to areas that are deemed to be 'safe' topics for at least minimally affluent consumer con-stituencies means that crucial issues are not tackled early enough. In addition, as Stole points out, CRM focuses on symptoms rather than core problems, providing, for example, tools for illiteracy rather than addressing the problem of funding for schools or economic inequality (Stole 2006).

More fundamentally, we might point out that CRM acts to help present corporations as the *saviours* of disastrous situations that they themselves contribute to causing. It is easy, for example, for a large corporation to improve their brand image and gain kudos by 'giving to Africa', but this can serve to bypass any role they have in generating and deepening patterns of poverty and the uneven global distribution of economic resources. Similarly, several feminist and environmental charities have critiqued the 'pink pro-ducts' sold for Breast Cancer Awareness because of the low level of donation to the charities in question, combined with the high degree to which these products contain and generate carcinogenic pollutants (Iggulden 2005). CRM has been made attractive to corporations because it is a tax-deductible expense: it already in effect is being subsidized by the public through tax breaks, which many businesses are pushing to extend further (Farquarson 2000; Charities Aid Foundation 2004). Moreover, CRM means that corpora-tions 'can present themselves as indispensable vehicles for social provision, enabling them to argue for a further reduction in state services' (Monbiot 2001). Put bluntly, it allows corporations to make very large claims about their social function – of their caring cosmopolitanism – without this func-tion being *accountable* to any significant degree. Stole argues that the CRM landscape now involves a risk that non-profits are having to potentially orient their work to be safer for such alignments with business, and that 'instead of risking such compromise, business should pay their fair share of taxes. Then, education, health care, research and other social priorities could receive greater funding, with no strings attached' (Stole 2006: 4).

By contrast, the benefits to the corporations' profits through such associations are far-reaching. Cause-related marketing is a variant of what Jim McGuigan (2006a) terms 'cool capitalism'; it functions as a low-cost form of brand leveraging which utilizes integrated emotional effect through its association with 'a good cause'. Through their mutual entrepreneurship with Product RED, American Express is therefore able to use cause-related marketing as a powerfully emotive and synergistic form of cross-promotion that is at the same time extremely cheap for the company to run. In industry interviews the company's Chief Marketing Officer John Hayes is frank about this aspect of the campaign, mainly because in this marketing context it becomes a read as a simple and unproblematic matter of achievement. He states: 'Because of its powerful marketing potential, we are not spending the same amount [on American Express RED] as we might have spent on a traditional product' (Silverman 2006). RED offers 'cumulative' forms of associative promotion across the combined range – so that 'American Express could benefit when someone wears a Red hooded sweatshirt from Gap or a pair of Red wraparound sunglasses from Emporio Armani' (Silverman 2006). Word of mouth and affective promotion is described as a huge potential marketing benefit of the campaign because of the relevance and emotional aspect or 'pull' factor of the subject matter. This very cross-promotional capacity, combined with Bono's association with the campaign, helped generate further media publicity about the brand (*The Independent* ran a special issue edited by Bono with a Product RED wraparound cover on the 16 May 2006).

The American Express campaign is a particularly salient example of cause-related marketing given that the global financial services company is often credited with launching the first instance of the practice through its 1983 marketing campaign for the Statue of Liberty Restoration project. One of the 30 corporations that are used to comprise the Dow Jones Industrial Average, American Express is ranked by Interbrand as the 14th most valuable brand in the world, and by business magazine *Fortune* as the 174th largest corporation.[6] Against this, its 1 per cent donation through product RED looks more than a little paltry given the amount of added value it reaps through related kudos and media publicity.

American Express's power has been fuelled by the revolution in and growth of the financial services industry over the past two decades, sometimes termed 'financialization' (Blackburn 2006).[7] This financial revolution has produced a context in which corporate scandals thrive, consumer investments such as pensions are increasingly vulnerable, and money is aggressively sought by Western-based financial services through entry into the 'emerging markets' of 'developing' countries (Glyn 2006). Indeed, as a recent *Financial Times* report pointed out, American Express has done particularly well in this area (Goff 2007). As Blackburn writes, such activities 'allow them to reap exceptional rates of return through repackaging the debts of the very poor. While Western governments boast of forgiving African debt,

Western banks get their hooks into loans to the poor' (Blackburn 2006: 45; see also Neff 1996).

American Express RED, we might say, marks the development of a highly productive marketing strategy that donates a small proportion to charity and helps absolve the conscience of its typically very wealthy consumer base. While it indicates how 'issues of global concern are becoming part of the everyday local experiences and the "moral life world" of the people (Beck 2002: 17), it also manifests a distinctly contemporary form of what Robbins and Cheang identified as an expression of elite right-wing cosmopolitanism; a form of right-wing cosmopolitan consumption which is being updated for the information age through the explicit use of the ideas of 'caring' and 'conscience'.

Islamic opposition: Mecca Cola and alternative consumer flows

> [T]he enormous potential of cosmopolitanism to politicise ... permeates the farthest reaches of world society and penetrates the capillaries of everyday life, goading people into public declarations and protest marches.
>
> (Beck 2006: 102)

Like RED Amex, Mecca Cola – a soft drink that has been marketed in Europe and the Middle East since 2002 – offers a form of caring cosmopolitan consumption with connections to charity. However, the economic and cultural forms of this particular model take quite different shapes and directions. 'Mecca', a city in Saudi Arabia, is well known as the holiest site of Islam, and Mecca Cola is marketed as a pro-Muslim drink. Some 10 per cent of its profits go towards funding 'humanitarian projects' in the Palestinian territories; and another 10 per cent goes to charities in the country the product is being sold in, more specifically to, as its MD, Tawfik Mathlouthi puts it, 'associations who work towards peace in the world and especially for peace in the conflict between Palestinians and fascist Zionist apartheid'.[8] Launched in Paris and now marketed across Europe, the Middle East, Asia and Africa, Mecca Cola works as a means to express – through consumption – cosmopolitan solidarity with various forms of global Islamic oppression. In addition, it functions like other drinks such as Zam Zam Cola in Iran (active since 1979) in that it offers consumers an alternative to that archetypal all-American product, Coca-Cola. Mathlouthi states that 'we are launching a new way of business ... a humanitarian business' in which 'our main aim is to be against Zionism and against American imperialism' (BBC2 2004).

Mecca Cola's anti-American discourse takes a somewhat different form to

many other strands of anti-Americanism which have until recently domi-
nated discussions in cultural studies; that is, of resentment towards a perceived or felt homogeneity of consumer environments (see Ritzer 2006), as it
explicitly defines itself against a perception of US-based warmongering
imperialism. In doing so, the brand is a reaction against the aggressive strategies of the George W. Bush administration in particular which has supported
the Israeli occupation of Palestine, invaded Iraq and bypassed transnational
modes of governance like the United Nations. This regime itself represents a
specific form of liberal cosmopolitanism in which the interests of neoconservative America are pronounced to be those of the world (Blackburn
2003; Gowan 2003; Harvey 2003).[9] 'Pax Americana' (the phrase used across
the political spectrum to signify a US-enforced, military imperialistic 'peace')
amounts, in Ulrich Beck's words, to the USA projecting itself as 'the hope of
the world' while attempting to 'replac[e] the United Nations by the United
States' (Beck 2006: 133) and to enforce itself as a global hegemon through
militaristic actions in Palestine and Iraq, actions which have simultaneously
alienated large swathes of the world's population.

In 'taking on' Coca-Cola, Mecca Cola has pitted itself against a staunchly
American drink which has attempted to market itself as quite a different kind
of cosmopolitan global product – most notoriously, through its landmark
1970s advertising campaign in which a group of people of 'different ethnicities' representing the world's population stand on a hill and harmonize the
song 'I'd like to teach the world to sing'. But the actual practices of the Coca-
Cola company have been less harmonious, and mired in controversy about
corporate abuses. Recently, for example, there have been demonstrations
against the company in Kerala, India, where it stands accused of polluting
water and poisoning land; and international protests over the company's
alleged complicity with human rights violations in Colombia, where trade
union officials have been murdered on Coca-Cola property while attempting
to negotiate collective agreements (see, for example, Rowell 2005). Coke's
culture has therefore also been perceived as participating in the same *liberal*
cosmopolitan discourse as the Bush administration, in which a narrative of
global interest is used as a strategy in driving distinctly American and specifically corporate interests. Indeed, the perceived correlation between
American imperialist foreign and economic policy, and neoliberal cosmopolitanism, is such that this process is sometimes described, in shorthand, as
'Coca-Colonisation' (Prendergast 1994). It is in relation to this discourse that
Mecca Cola situates itself: it attempts to harness an American consumer tide
and subvert its message, turn it back against itself by creating an oppositional
consumer product.

In this respect, Mecca Cola is a 'buycott': an oppositional or 'anti' product
that is promoted as the alternative to a brand that is being avoided for reasons
of wider social purpose. Buycotts have a long history. They range from the

Swadeshi, or 'buy Indian' movement, which was central to Gandhi's strategy for Indian independence in the early part of the twentieth century to, more recently, the purchase of dolphin-friendly tuna and Palestinian branded olive oil (Gabriel and Lang 1995: 163–72; Micheletti 2003: 48). Effectively, the buycott is a consumer act that integrates the *boycott* of one type of brand or good (or consumer 'striking'), with the *purchase* of another.[10] Purposely produced 'buycott' products therefore often become a medium of political mobilization, and also – particularly when they are in the least bit noteworthy, controversial or visually conspicuous, as in the case of Mecca Cola – become a form of what would now be known as 'ambient marketing' for the message.

But what exactly *is* its message? We might say that by pitting itself against the globalizing Americanization of Coca-Cola, Mecca Cola has presented itself as making an intervention in the work of redefining global trade flows: to attempt to push them in an alternative direction. It appears to manifest an oppositional form of cosmopolitanism, a global cultural ware that pits itself against Pax Americana. Mike Featherstone argues that since 11 September, 'the world has become increasingly divided into friends and enemies with the main enemy increasingly constructed, following the lead of Samuel Huntington (1996) and Francis Fukuyama (1992) as "Islam" ' (Featherstone 2002: 14). But as a host of commentators, including Featherstone, have pointed out, accounts of a 'clash of civilisations' in the type of discourse Huntington deploys are deeply reductive, as they present civilizations, and ethnicities, as 'natural', solid and historically immutable categories, rather than porous, malleable and open to change (Huntington 1996; McGuigan 2005). As Edward Said (2001) eloquently put it, such essentialized versions of ethnicity are 'better for reinforcing defensive self-pride than for critical understanding of the bewildering interdependence of our time'. One question to ask of Mecca Cola's alternative, then, is to what extent does it *replicate* such a reductive template of ethnic-religious essentialisms by merely inverting it? To what extent is its 'cosmopolitan vision' limited in this way?

In other words, does Mecca Cola reproduce the binary structure that Benjamin Barber characterizes as 'Jihad vs McWorld' (Barber 2003) by solidifying a category of Islamic culture and leaning towards a 'closed' form of cultural essentialism? Pointing out that, both in the Arab states and across the world, recent Islamist movements have become increasingly essentialist, Asef Bayat (2003) argues that recent Islamist movements have

> rendered the Arab states more religious (as states moved to rob Islamism of its moral authority), more nativist or nationalist (as states moved to assert their Arab authenticity and to disown democracy as a Western construct) and more repressive, since the liquidation of radical Islamists offered states the opportunity to control other forms of dissent.

Yet for Bayat, the most progressive activities in this context are precisely the new 'grassroots charity and boycotts, or product campaigns' offered as mediums of political mobilization. Bayat therefore locates Mecca Cola together with a range of other examples, including students at the American University in Cairo taking 30 250-ton truckloads of charitable products to Palestinians in Gaza in 2002, and the actions of 'millions of Arabs and Muslims' in 'boycotting American and Israeli products, including McDonald's, KFC, Starbucks, Nike and Coca-Cola' (Bayat 2003). Bayat highlights these activities as valuable and not as repressive as other strands of contemporary Islamic activity because, first, they are perceived as being 'grassroots' in their nature and as not being directed by an increasingly authoritarian state; and, second, because they are perceived as being *transnational*.

Bayat's opinion is that Mecca Cola is part of a wider, more contemporary, forward-looking means of resisting Western neo-imperialism. This is echoed by how, in World Social Forums – the large meetings of left, green and anti-imperialist NGOs, activists and campaigners who come together to exchange ideas about alter-globalization or how to imagine that 'another world is possible' – Mecca Cola has often featured as *the* drink of choice on sale, bought by a wide range of non-Muslims. Mecca Cola was also one of the sponsors of the 2003 anti-Iraq war rallies in Britain; and Mathlouthi has spoken of his desire to expand the brand into Latin America, specifically Venezuela and Argentina: to 'other countries that are fed up with American hegemony, and not only Muslim countries'.[11] These examples serve to foreground the *extent* and the *range* of the alliances and connections that are being made to Mecca Cola in particular and to internationalist Islam in general, as a response to what is perceived as Western imperialism.

These connections can also be situated in more general terms, as the link between international political Islam and anti-American imperialism has a long history: we might think, for example, of how certain strands of the black power struggles of the 1970s identified with elements of Islam against 'western imperialism', particularly through the figure of Malcolm X (Malcolm X, Haley with Gilroy 2001). Today this articulation has a distinctly contemporary inflection. As Hisham Aidi (2003) puts it:

> Over the past two years, Islam has provided an anti-imperial idiom and imaginary community of belonging for many subordinate groups in the West, as Islamic culture and art stream into the West through minority and diaspora communities, and often in fusion with African-American art forms, slowly seep into the cultural mainstream. Subsequently, many of the cultural and protest movements – anti-globalization, anti-imperialist, anti-racist – in the West today have Islamic and/or African-American undercurrents. At a time of military conflict and extreme ideological polarization between the

West and the Muslim world, Islamic culture is permeating political and cultural currents, remaking identities and creating cultural linkages between Westerners and the Muslim world.

In effect, this describes what we might term as a cultural diaspora of anti-Western imperialism, one that draws on political Islam as one form of sustenance (the widespread popularity of the keffiyeh headscarf is one good example). The connections being made between 'anti-Western imperialism' and 'Islam' are therefore adopting a specific contemporary inflection in relation to the current context of US imperialism. Simultaneously, they have the potential to adopt quite a broad range of forms – forms that can often be quite different in their ideological focus and in the way they are translated and used. In this sense, contemporary Islamic-oriented anti-US imperialisms have an equivalence to nationalist post-colonial movements in terms of the wide range of politics they can entail.

In relation to this wide political spectrum, it is worth thinking about exactly what 'alternative' Mecca produces on economic terms. Mecca Cola's business is clearly economically tiny in comparison to the gargantuan proportions of the Coca-Cola corporation. Even while the remarkable success of alternative products 'has caused Coca-Cola to lose some 20 to 40 percent of its market share in some countries' (Aidi 2003), Coke has not to date sued Mecca Cola for infringing its copyright, even though Mecca's red and white logo directly imitates Coca-Cola's. As Mark Prendergast, author of a cultural history of Coke points out, this is both because the smaller company is simply not enough of a threat, and because suing them would simply generate positive publicity for Mecca, making Coca-Cola look like the evil Goliath attempting to crush their saintly 'David'-like rival (BBC2 2004).

Mecca Cola's *image* is primarily one which emphasizes being 'politically caring' and distances itself from the 'corporate'. This was highlighted in a BBC TV programme *Message in a Bottle,* which documented Mecca Cola's business strategy in relation to a new British rival, Qibla Cola. In this programme, Qibla was presented as the more sleek and polished company – with an experienced branding and marketing team – against which Mecca was the shambolically disorganized organization, employing its staff for their political principles rather than business acumen. In retrospect, this programme is particularly interesting, first, because, despite the slick and effective image of Qibla in the programme, the company collapsed in 2005, and, second, because Mecca Cola was presented, in imagistic terms, as not particularly commercially oriented. And it needs to be pointed out that whatever its *effectiveness*, Mecca Cola is not a co-operative (like, for example, the Palestinian Olive Co-operative). Mecca Cola is run as a capitalist organization; but as a specific type of capitalist organization, in that it gives a large slice of its profits – 20 per cent – to charity.[12] In effect, Mecca Cola's strategy might be viewed as an Islamic variant on corporate social responsibility – an issue I explore in the next chapter – as it is a commercial company that both uses some of its profits to intervene in social problems and uses such intervention as a marketing strategy for the company.

This practice can be further understood by positioning it in the larger context of how over the past few decades one very powerful strand of political Islam has increasingly been rendered compatible with capital accumulation (Rodinson 1974; Blackburn 2003: 143–5). This tendency runs from the form of the power of the profoundly autocratic 'state-owned' corporations that are powerful in Saudi Arabia and Dubai, and which are supported by the Bush administration, to a more general linkage between an Islamist message and corporate values distributed to a wider audience through such mechanisms as schools of economics (Roy 1996, quoted in Blackburn 2003: 157). Given this context, it is telling that Mecca Cola relocated to the centre of Middle Eastern autocratic corporate capitalism, Dubai, from France.

There is a very long and rich history of post-colonial activism and academic work that emphasizes imperialism's role in the looting of other countries' resources and as such in the generation of capital (see, for example, Hall 1992, 1998). In a contemporary context, commentators such as David Harvey and the Retort collective (among others) have discussed how a new round of 'primitive accumulation' is being pushed by the neoconservative US government, through, for instance, their scramble to control Iraqi oil (Harvey 2005; Retort 2005). The neoliberal drive to extend corporate capital is in these terms constitutive of the neoconservative agenda of the Bush government; a formation David Harvey explicitly labels *The New Imperialism* (Harvey 2003). Mecca Cola does not participate in this particular tradition of unravelling the economic and political interconnections of imperialism. It is critical of American dominance, but not of the economic logic shaping US neoliberalism. Mecca Cola, we might say, operates as an anti-imperialist endeavour that does not confront the interconnections between imperialism and capitalism.

Mecca Cola then symbolizes both a distinctly contemporary and profoundly ambiguous form of cosmopolitanism. It has established a cultural image of being 'against' US neo-imperialism or the 'Pax Americana' version of liberal cosmopolitanism. It is a consumer form of internationalist political Islam which is used to make *wider* cosmopolitan alliances outside Islam and to make connections to other anti-Bush sentiments as well as to anti-capitalist agendas. Yet it is clearly a corporation rather than a co-operative, and therefore in economic terms is structurally akin to American Express, only on a much smaller level. Where there are vast differences between the American Express RED campaign and Mecca Cola are over anti-American imperialist sentiment and the scale of the corporate giving – American Express's 1 per cent as opposed to Mecca Cola's 20 per cent.

Such a comparison also demonstrates how the vast majority of corporate cause-related marketing activity (as in the case of American Express RED) tend to deal with subjects deemed 'safe': it is more than a little hard to envisage American Express supporting Palestinian charities at the present moment. Mecca is different to American Express RED in this regard because it is not only an instance of cause-related marketing but because it is also a political 'buycott'. The declared aims of the product and its purpose (as a counter-weight to US products) are, in Mecca Cola's case, much more congruent with the charities (primarily Palestinian humanitarian organizations) than American Express RED (i.e. between a global financial services company based in the USA and AIDS relief in Africa). While buycotts such as Gandhi's Swadeshi movement were part of the campaign 'for' nationalism and 'against' British imperialism, and buycotts of dolphin-friendly tuna are part of the campaign 'for' globalized environmental standards and 'against' the unnecessary slaughter of dolphins, Mecca Cola is part of a quasi-globalized campaign 'for' an alternative to US-oriented neo-imperialism, one with an ambiguous relationship to consumer capitalism and a reach beyond the Islamic culture it seeks to augment. It is partly this very ambiguity – an ambiguity particularly apparent in its visuals – which makes Mecca Cola such a powerful media icon with a large discursive reach. We might summarize this form of cosmopolitanism as an Islamic anti-imperialist cosmopolitanism, expansive in its challenge and somewhat problematically limited in its solutions.

Addressing the activist-consumer: Make Trade Fair

> To be a cosmopolitan now is no longer to feel oneself a citizen *of* the world but also, and above all, a citizen *for* the world.
>
> (Archibugi 2003: 264)

The third instance of 'cosmopolitan caring consumption' I want to consider is the increasing imbrication of fair trade with activist-oriented campaigning over globalization. To do this, I look at the campaign developed by the British wing of the international charity Oxfam, Make Trade Fair, initially rolled out over 2001/2 and ongoing at the time of writing, which marked a shift in the way the international charity dealt with fair trade. The broader landscape of fair trade has become increasingly diverse over the past decade, both through the marked expansion of fair trade foodstuffs in North America, Japan and especially Europe (in the UK, for example, the number of products sold increased by 90 per cent between 2000 and 2002) and diversification into different niche markets (Co-operative Bank 2003; Fairtrade Foundation 2003; Nicholls and Opal 2005). For example, the marketing of fair trade products ranges from presenting it as hedonistic quasi-exoticism (such as Cafédirect's rebranding of itself around lush landscapes), through encouraging children to be what we might call 'cheerful connectors' (such as the Dubble chocolate bar, aimed at kids) or through a more directly religious discourse of help (such as the Christian fair trade charity Traidcraft). Emerging out of this context, Oxfam's particular intervention has been to address what we might call an 'activist-consumer': someone who would both buy fair trade and campaign to change global trade rules.

While Oxfam's work has long involved intervening in questions of international trade and political and economic policy, the charity – initially founded in Oxford in the UK in the 1940s to aid famine – has traditionally been well known for addressing mainly affluent, white, middle-aged, middle-class liberals (Black 1992). This particular campaign made a specific intervention into the politics of the contemporary globalization debates and adopted a style and rhetoric more usually associated with direct action protestors. Make Trade Fair encouraged both the buying of fair trade and campaigning against global trade rules, addressing, in the process, an 'activist consumer'. This youthful and energetic approach has since been extended in the later campaign that has run alongside it, Make Poverty History. Make Trade Fair's specific campaign aims have included: the democratization of the WTO to 'give poorer countries a stronger voice'; an end to the conditions imposed by the IMF-World Bank programmes which force 'developing' countries to open up their markets and governments to privatize essential services; and the reform of intellectual property rules to ensure that workers in poorer countries are not prohibited from swapping such fundamental goods as seed and can afford basic technology (Oxfam 2002a, 2002b). Outlining these objectives, Oxfam used strident rhetoric to argue that '[t]he existing trade system is indefensible and unsustainable' and therefore that Make Trade Fair 'aims to change world trade rules' (Oxfam 2002b). As one campaign worker put it: 'the campaign ... is responding to globalisation and trends that mean international trade impacts on developing countries in a negative way' (Wood 2003).

The majority of the campaign's aims are shared by many of the different interest groups in the alter-globalization 'movement of movements', which has created alternative world summits to the WTO trade talks in the form of 'world social forums'. The movement which burgeoned after the 'Battle of Seattle' protests in 1999 at the WTO Ministerial trade talks escalated levels of public debate about the processes of globalization (see, for example, Klein 2000, 2002; Shepard and Hayduk 2002; Notes from Nowhere 2003; Wainwright 2003; Mertes 2004; Gilbert 2008) and has been composed of people and groups of varying political persuasions (who often, notoriously, disagree) but who predominantly share the commonality of attempting to rethink and create processes of globalization that might be more participatory (or in the strapline of the social forums, to attempt to think how 'another world is possible'). Drawing on this alter-globalization discourse was a conscious strategy of Make Trade Fair. As Alison Woodhead, the Campaign Manager told me, 'we felt the time was right to enter this debate: Seattle had made it timely' (interview, Woodhead 2004; Oxfam 2004).

Make Trade Fair's posters, website and associated materials use a visual aesthetic which attempt to appeal to the immediacy of activism, targeted in particular (though not exclusively) at a 18–25 age group. The use of 'ambient' marketing to this age group in the campaign has taken the form of tailored promotional products such as temporary tattoos that were given away at Glastonbury Music Festival and Notting Hill Carnival.[13] Its imagery inter-pellates a consumer who already has some existing sense of unequal trade dynamics and who will be sympathetic to an approach that appears to be making an *immediate* intervention. Its graphics are blunt, noisy and high-impact. No-nonsense directness is conveyed by imagery that isolates and amplifies particular aspects of the activist-consumer's projected experience (spitting out coffee, or making a 'big noise' through a loudspeaker), or uses high-impact puns (a cracked mug denoting the 'cracked' logic of interna-tional trading rules). Such performances of directness, combined with the rough-cut 'homemade' appearance of the stencilled typography and collage are redolent of the punk and Situationist-derived graphics used by envir-onmentalist and anti-capitalist groups such as Reclaim the Streets (see Jordan 1998; Soar 2002). By performing directness through stark language and imagery, Make Trade Fair has carved out a differently nuanced promotional identity to that of Oxfam's core branding, which has a 'softer' visual identity and gentler message ('you can help').[14]

While Make Trade Fair functioned as a targeted niche marketing cam-paign with its own distinct identity within Oxfam's overall communications mix, it also indicated a change of strategy in response to the expanding fair trade market which had not only increased rapidly in terms of size, but also in terms of widespread supermarket availability in the UK in the early 2000s. This meant that the majority of consumers buying fair trade had been able to 'mainstream' purchases of fair trade into their regular shopping trip rather than go out of their way to source products from a 'specialist' outlet (Co-operative Bank 2003; Fairtrade Foundation 2003) although such new levels of availability simultaneously involved fair trade being channelled through the distinctly dubious ethical practices of supermarket conglomerates (see, for example, Simms 2007). In response to this context, Oxfam halted production of its own-label fair trade produce, instead selling goods sourced by other organizations (such as Equal Exchange and Traidcraft) through its shops and website and channelled a larger amount of resources into campaigns pro-moting fair trade on a different levels (Townsend 2003).

In other words, Make Trade Fair combined a strategy of encouraging consumers to buy fair trade goods and at the same time to campaign to change global trade rules: *buying* fair trade was positioned as but one part of the social marketing mix. Its promotional material, for instance, encourages ways to get involved with Oxfam's campaigning, stating that '[i]t's important to buy fair trade, but taking action to help poor farmers to get a decent price for their crop is just as vital'. In this way, it emphasizes the authority of the consumer as an agent who is potentially able to contribute directly to broader social change through a variety of actions, both through and beyond consumption. Such attempts to reform global trade in favour of more equitable global distribution of resources mark it out as a more left-wing form of cosmopolitanism than the American Express RED campaign.

It is worth considering the campaign's imagery in this context, as it indicates both some of the expansiveness and limitations of its mode of cosmopolitanism. There is an increasing understanding in many NGOs/ NFPs[15] dealing with issues of global trade and poverty that overtly imperialistic imagery could easily be read as patronizing and not 'play' so well to younger constituencies in particular (Stein 2003). Make Trade Fair is a very striking example of this trend; while, as Oxfam's Marketing Manager pointed out, 'our trading division still produce some glossy materials in support of fair trade which is much more traditional, with beautiful pictures and smiling producers' (interview, Woodhead 2004). In the imagery of Make Trade Fair it is possible to discern a discursive shift: from the interpellation of consumers for whom buying a fair trade product was an act of quasi-imperial charity towards an 'other' world, towards, to some extent, quasi-activist campaigning consumers who are imagined as occupying a more or less shared spatial and temporal context in a global village.

For instance, one of the promotional images used depicts a blonde white woman holding a coffee mug and grimacing with distaste, the phrase 'What's that in your coffee?' stencilled in bold capitals above her. Inside the leaflet, we are told what is in the coffee:

> Poverty and misery for coffee growers, massive profits for the big coffee companies. Don't swallow it. … But when you choose a Fair trade marked brand, you know that the farmers who grow it get a better deal – a fair price for their crop and opportunities to gain the skills and knowledge to help develop their business.
>
> (Oxfam 2002a)

This advert works as a pun to 'defetishize' a global commodity by rendering the exploitation of the means of production metaphorically palpable in the product itself, in which the 'bitterness' of the coffee emerges by tasting the exploitation, in which the meaning of 'bitterness' shifts from sensory perception of taste to a conceptual category of disgust. It works, in Marxist terms, as a critique of reification. Or, to look at it another way, it dramatizes actor-network theory (ANT), a system of thought used to consider how objects are not simply 'used' by humans but are themselves 'actants' putting events and possibilities in motion (see Law and Hassard 1999). For instance, Bruno Latour writes of how the hammer which he picks up from his workbench

> keeps folded heterogeneous temporalities, one of which has the antiquity of the planet, because of the mineral from which it has been moulded, while another has the age of the oak which provided the handle, while still another has the age of the 10 years since it came out of the German factory which produced it for the market. When I grab the handle, I insert my gesture in 'a garland of time'.
>
> (Latour 2002: 249)

To adapt these terms, what is in the mug are the heterogeneous temporalities of the coffee, including its less aesthetically pleasing moments: from the coffee beans being sprayed with pesticide, through their harvesting by exploited producers, to being owned and doused in hot water by a consumer. These temporalities co-exist in the mug and are 'unfolded' by the advert. The coffee is presented as not just objectified matter put into motion by humans, but as an 'actant' which itself sets events and possibilities in motion, which could reconfigure 'global' or planetary 'geometries of power' (Gilroy 2000; Massey 2002).

Make Trade Fair, therefore, enfolds a particular kind of story about existing social relations and future possibilities: or what Arjun Appadurai describes as a 'mediascape'; 'image-centred, narrative-based accounts of strips of reality', which

> offer to those who experience and transform them ... a series of elements (such as characters, plots, and textual forms) out of which scripts can be formed of imagined lives, their own as well as those of others living in other places. These scripts can and do get dis-aggregated into complex sets of metaphors by which people live (Lakoff and Johnson 1980) as they help to constitute narratives of the Other and protonarratives of possible lives.
>
> (Appadurai 1996: 35–6)

The Make Trade Fair script offers its audience a relatively expansive cosmo-politanism through the experience of imagining themselves someone exist-ing in the same temporarility as 'others', namely exploited producers in faraway places; and of themselves as consumers and active, activist-like agents who have the power to say 'no' to such bitter exploitation. It segues with Couze Venn's argument that temporality has to be key to any ethics of cos-mopolitanism; 'the knowledge that we exist as beings in time makes time itself the highest, irreducible, value' and so should be the means through which 'responsibility for the other' can be generalized in the public sphere (Venn 2002: 78).

In drawing on the style and message of alter-globalization movements, Make Trade Fair's activist-consumer can therefore be thought of as broadening the appeal of such discourses. This is particularly the case as sometimes the celebration of a kind of 'purity' of activism can give it a mythic force which, while potent and generative, can also exclude a wide range of people without particular forms of social and cultural capital from identifying with it, as I explore in Chapter 4. The types of identification that fair trade activists have can often work in slightly different ways to those upon which other alter-globalization campaigns rely, facilitating more alliances; as people often don't join fair trade action groups but rather incorporate it into their 'everyday lives', by switching their office, for example, to fair trade produce (Timms 2004).

However, in other ways the campaign's cosmopolitan vision is more limited. For example, 'What's that in your coffee?' featured two women – one blonde, one brunette (both Oxfam employees in the Netherlands, where the advertising agency produced the images) spitting out the bitter coffee into their mugs. The imagined conceptual horizons of the project are restricted to the imperial dynamics of depicting only white European women as potential consumer activists. In this sense, its 'script' is not so radically democratic as might be hoped. In addition, the Eurocentricism of the campaign become apparent when Oxfam belatedly realized that the spitting featuring in the images the campaign 'was considered offensive in some African cultures' (interview, Woodhead 2004). This prompted reassessment of the cultural bias within sections of the campaign, and consequently, they 'glocalized' sections of the materials. This is an instance of what Appadurai describes as a 'disjuncture' between mediascapes – a moment when different meanings emerge in a media narrative as it travels – and of a moment when the restricted nature of the campaign's cosmopolitanism was realized and acted on. As Woodhead put it, 'It was a real eye-opener in terms of the realities ... that you can't just produce one set of materials. The campaign is global but parts of it need to be done locally. It has to be different in Mozambique than London' (interview, Woodhead 2004).

Interestingly, these factors have in part been addressed in more recent campaigns on fair trade and global poverty by both Oxfam and other NGOs who are increasingly taking pains to be more aware of diverging global audiences as well as to interpelate 'western' consumers as black and Asian as well as white. But such disjunctures also prompt larger questions about the limits of 'planetary mutuality' or shared empowerment in fair trade (and NGO) discourses. It is clearly still the case that a relatively privileged section of fair trade consumers hold more power than the producers. This means that for critics like Matthias Zick Varul, for example, fair trade itself is a failure in its own terms. He argues that while fair trade 'defetishizes' the global commodity chains that are typically obscured through capitalist commodification (which conventionally circulate around the properties of the commodity), and thereby tries to move away from the paternalistic implications of charity, fair trade also perpetuates charity through a new kind of symbolic value and works both to compensate for and to 'develop the moral grammar of capitalism' by romanticizing and re-fetishizing *producers* in the South, and their labour, for the benefit of consumers in the North. While his argument tends to downplay the material significance of the safety blanket of fair trade for producers against harsher forms of global capitalism, and the significance of fair trade's role in supporting co-operatives (see Barrat Brown 1993), this is a powerful point.[16]

But if Make Trade Fair fetishizes the labour of producers for the benefit of Northern consumers, it also finds ways of moving beyond what Varul characterizes as 'consumer power as a means of global governance' by encouraging the consumer to also become an activist, to campaign to change global trade rules, or, by bringing into being a hybrid 'activist consumer'. In this sense, it offers a more far-reaching opportunity to intervene in global inequalities than American Express RED (as well as offering a more left-wing type of cosmopolitanism). But equally, this means we need to interrogate the type of activist campaigning that the charity is engaged in. Simultaneously, charities and NGOs are often described today as an arch example of actually existing cosmopolitanism or 'cosmopolitanization' (Beck 2006: 93). Luc Boltanski has described the rise of NGOs over the past 20 years as 'an alternative cosmopolitan force', a nascent 'humanitarian movement' whose 'consolidation depends, at least in part, on its ability to clarify and make explicit the connection, which is often realized in practice by its members, between distant causes and the traditions, sensibilities and even interests of those who organize support for these causes' (Boltanski 1999: xiv). These connections are what Make Trade Fair – with its shared temporalities between activist-consumers and exploited producers – is engaging with.

They also show clearly how the landscape has shifted, for example, since John Hutnyk wrote *The Rumour of Calcutta* in the mid-1990s, when the imperialistic discourse within charity aid was predominantly much more explicitly focused on pity, and those NGO workers or charity discourses which even gestured towards tackling questions of debt seemed relatively unusual, or far-reaching (Hutnyk 1996: 76–7). And yet a rigorously critical approach, as Gayatri Spivak reminds us in *Cosmopolitics,* also needs to question these newer forms of contemporary cosmopolitanism. For,

> [t]he great narrative of Development is not dead ... Many of the
> functionaries of the civilizing mission were well-meaning: but alas,
> you can do good with contempt or paternal-maternal-sororal

> benevolence in your heart. And today, you can knife the poor nation
> in the back and offer Band-Aids for a photo opportunity.
>
> (Spivak 1998: 332–3)

More specifically, it needs to be asked if there are any limitations with the types of cosmopolitanism projected and promoted by NGOs and charities such as Oxfam. Pheng Cheah in *Cosmopolitics*, for instance, has gestured towards the problem of 'strings-attached funding to elite NGOs' (Cheah 1998: 31).[17] One example here is how in 2003 the US wing of the international charity Save the Children received funding from the Bush government, which led to the UK wing being ordered to stop criticizing US policy in Iraq (Macguire 2003). However, the wider point is, as Cheah puts it, not to slip into a stance of simply dismissing the work of every intervention including NGOs, but rather 'to look at the consequences of cosmopolitan claims in a given historical situation' (Cheah 1998: 31).

And here, other arguments emerge as to why Oxfam's cosmopolitan vision itself might be somewhat limited; for the problems occurring in the global travels of the advertising image, which highlighted its cultural specificity and white Euro-centricism, were also symptomatic of wider problems with the campaign. These issues surfaced as Oxfam's sister campaign to Make Trade Fair, Make Poverty History, became increasingly prominent in 2005 as the key banner under which a broader coalition of charities and non-profit organizations seeking to address the poverty and debt of the world's poorest countries came together, receiving large swathes of media attention (see Nash 2008).[18] As Priya Gopal points out, the humanitarian narratives circulating around it marked genuine progress for three reasons: first, it marked a shift from a rhetoric of 'enlightened self-interest' to global shared interests; second, it cautiously acknowledged that poverty reduction is an issue of 'justice' rather than 'charity'; and third, it showed – however weakly – that politics and economics are not separate entities and that human agency is necessary to effect change.

Yet as Gopal argues, narratives of 'justice' can be at one and the same time both a constructive step and destructively shallow in their use: for while Make Poverty History

> brought tens of thousands of young people to at least a minimal awareness of 'Third World debt' and so-called free trade as issues … there is also no doubt that the very success of th[e] mobilization has relied on a discursive enactment of concern accompanied by an insistent and comforting disavowal of material implication.
>
> (Gopal 2006: 97)

Simultaneously, a number of commentators pointed out that Make Poverty History also had become somewhat elided with a Blairite agenda, close to the UK election, of 'helping' developing countries, particularly Africa, while promoting processes of privatization benefiting Western multinationals; and thereby entrenching new forms of inequality and exploitation (Townsend 2005). As one journalist put it, the 'finger is being pointed at Oxfam, the UK's biggest development organization, for allowing the movement's demands to be diluted and the message to become virtually indistinguishable from that of the government' (Quarmby 2005). In other words, Make Poverty History utilized the myth of economic growth as a solution to grinding poverty, which was imagined as being able to be accessed once a few reforms were out of the way. In doing so, the campaign often, though not uniformly, deployed a discourse of corporate globalization and neoimperalism (Gopal 2006: 91–7).

As Make Poverty History rose to prominence, Make Trade Fair became subsumed into it as part of its campaign. The mixed involvement of Make Trade Fair with both contemporary forms of anti-capitalism and, at the same time with furthering the interests of the UK government in providing more opportunities for multinationals in 'developing' countries is therefore profoundly ambiguous. It gestures at one and the same time to the possibilities of anti-corporate imagery being used to perpetuate the interest of corporations and to the enormous possibilities inherent in the linkages between different interest groups which have been kept apart.

Conclusion: an expansion of participatory positions?

> We live in a world of what I like to call 'overlapping communities of fate' where the trajectories of countries are heavily emeshed with each other.
>
> (Held 2003: 185)

In *The Spectacle of Suffering*, Lille Chouliarki discusses the various different subject positions that are made available to us as TV viewers watching global catastrophes. Chouliarki finds the options we are given as viewer-participators to be profoundly limited. This limited range is symptomatic of a 'crisis of pity' which 'is inextricably linked with the history of western public life and, specifically, with the narrow repertoire of participatory positions that this public life makes available for the ordinary citizen' (Chouliarki 2006: 10). But in contemporary cosmopolitan caring consumption a wider range of participatory subject positions appear to be emerging. In particular, there are an increasing number of ways in which as a consumer we are being encouraged to move beyond an explicit model of what Luc Boltanski (after Hannah Arendt) terms 'the politics of pity' and towards 'the politics of justice'

(Boltanski 1999: 3–54). There are products to buy, like Mecca Cola, which allow us to register an alternative to current US imperialism. Donating to charity, as through American Express RED, can be done without mobilizing guilt, but rather by making us feel like we're having fun while choosing to be ethical. We can join in with the Make Trade Fair project and buy products that give faraway producers a better wage than they would have otherwise received and campaign to change the rules of the political-economic game. The possibilities of how we might be caring and cosmopolitan appear to be widening through these contemporary developments in consumption.

However, at the same time the forms of 'justice' on offer are not always as far-reaching as they want to be, and there is an expansion in the possibilities to create or *augment* new kinds of global inequalities through cosmopolitan 'caring' consumption. The charity donation through consumption vastly extends the power of organizations that make their profits through the exploitation of the global poor. The alternative to US imperialism cannot offer much beyond a resistant consumer project that reproduces much of its economic model in miniature. The fair trade campaign ends up reiterating some quasi-imperialist sentiments and structures even while campaigning to reform them.

If types of what I term here 'cosmopolitan caring consumption' therefore make a variety of different interventions, then, they also prompt questions about how these interventions could be better. There are clearly broader aspects of what we might call 'progressive practice' at work here. The movement towards a rhetoric of 'justice' rather than pity, the encouragement of innovative new forms of co-operatives, the potential for coalitions or articulations to be made across the world and between different interest groups, the mobilization of a wider range of affective engagements with consumer and producer justice, and the capacity for consumption to link with movements beyond consumer governance are all elements which fall into that category. The challenge is to think about how such specific elements could be pushed further.

In these terms, we might say that Mecca Cola, for example, would be a more far-reaching alternative to Coca-Cola if it explored co-operative production; that Oxfam needs to engage more deeply with the broader rules of economic trading if it really wants to make trade fair; that American Express RED might perhaps contribute to lessening rather than sustaining inequalities if it was forced to contribute a much higher percentage to anti-AIDS charities and if its international investment activities were much more stringently regulated; or that, even more effectively, the potential RED consumer could instead open a Co-operative Bank account and donate to an anti-AIDS charity. But evaluating how cosmopolitan caring consumption could be more effective not only involves thinking about how it could improve: it also involves understanding the character of what is stopping it from doing so. It is therefore to the question of corporate power, and to one of the most controversial strategies through which we are currently encouraged to believe that consumption can be rendered more ethical – corporate social responsibility – to which the next chapter turns.

3 Greenwash, whitewash, hogwash?

CSR and the media management of consumer concern

CSR is a commitment to improve community well-being through discretionary business practices and contributions of resources.
(Kotler and Lee 2006: 3)

Christian Aid defines Corporate Social Responsibility – CSR – as an entirely voluntary, corporate-led initiative to promote self-regulation as a substitute for regulation at either national or international level.
(Christian Aid 2004: 5)

Kiss my bottom line.
(Slogan on activist banner at a 2006 UK rally against current CSR laws)[1]

'Corporate social responsibility' (CSR) is a phrase that has rocketed into public prominence over the past decade. First used as a term in the 1970s, it became popular in the 1990s to indicate corporate attempts to show that their operations and actions were socially and environmentally responsible, ethical and sustainable. Today, CSR encompasses a gamut of activities, from annual audits demonstrating a company's attempts to minimize its negative effects on the environment and communities, to 'programmes' in which corporations show themselves to be engaged in charitable activities and community projects. But, as the wildly varying quotes above indicate, there is no agreement as to what CSR 'actually means': on the contrary, there is often furious disagreement and contradiction. To some, CSR is simply a con, a marketing confidence trick, in which corporations 'whitewash' their tarnished image to avoid being associated with labour exploitation or human rights abuses – or use tokenistic eco projects to 'greenwash' their brand name in an age of anxiety over global warming. To others it is a means by which corporations aim to 'give something back' to the society and community they are part of. To others again, it is viewed as a necessary brake on corporate power and one of the only realistic routes to a more equitable mode of consumption. It is easy, for instance, to imagine how the GAP's recent declarations of 'responsible' practices – which mean that the company is now being endorsed by the Ethical Trading Initiative, while still coming under fire for its use of child labour – could be interpreted in any or all of these ways.[2]

In other words, we might say that we are witnessing a struggle over the discursive terrain of 'corporate social responsibility': that there is a contest of meaning in process, a fight over what CSR indicates; over whether it even exists; or if it is simply a contradiction in terms. Questions about CSR in an academic context have predominantly – indeed, overwhelmingly – remained sequestered in business studies, where the primary debate is over whether or not it is a profitable strategy to be implemented by companies (for example, Hopkins 2003, 2007; Henderson 2004; Henriques and Richardson 2004; Kotler and Lee 2006; Henriques 2007) and in this context, the parameters of the discussion – however varied the contents of the discussions themselves might be – tend to be both delimited and fixed by the underlying question of how, and to what extent, its various forms are *good for business*.

By contrast, this chapter takes a very different approach: both by having as an underlying premise the need to hold open the question of to what extent CSR is good for culture and society, and by approaching the subject of CSR from a different angle by drawing on cultural and media studies and cultural theory. For a key feature of CSR, as I explore here, is its extensive and multiple promotional role and its forceful, synergistic function as a media strategy, and investigating these points can provide an alternative account of its rise. This chapter therefore suggests that CSR can be considered as a form of media management which corporations use as both an external and internal means of communication, through which it acts as a mechanism to intervene in and to attempt to regulate some of the forms of consumer concern over environmental, social and cultural contexts of production) that we have already looked at.

This chapter is therefore less concerned with the question of shareholder profit, or with the media mechanics of its implementation (which so preoccupy business texts) than with the question of *why* and *how* CSR has evolved as a strategy in the contemporary cultural landscape. By delving into the promotional character of CSR as a form of media management, it shows how CSR might both be located in a longer historical context and understood as an updated version of corporate philanthropy for what theorists such as Manuel Castells have termed our 'information age' (Castells 1996). In tracing these developments, it also participates in an expanding body of work on the reconfigurations of contemporary promotional culture (for a good summary, see Davis 2005).

I begin by outlining some of the various different perspectives on CSR, offering a brief sketch of four positions that are, variously, pro-/anti-CSR and/ or pro/anti-corporate, and highlighting the range and complexity of different political stances it is possible to take on the subject. The chapter then moves on to locate CSR in the broader context of histories of corporate philan-thropy, corporate welfare and promotional culture. It shows how CSR can be understood in terms of longer histories of both the corporate channelling of producer/consumer desire for social change, and of traditions of persuasion and media management; and, simultaneously, as a distinctly contemporary *twist* on these traditions, one entailing a specific fusion between them. It then develops these themes by discussing the little-discussed 'internal' commu-nication features of CSR, relating this to Eva Illouz's conception of a new contemporary 'communication episteme' and to the recent emergence of participatory modes of production, or what Robin Murray calls 'post-post-Fordism'. Lastly, the chapter uses this contextual understanding to open up questions about CSR's relationship to regulation, which, it argues, might today be more thoroughly reconceived as the ways we regulate ourselves as a culture and society, rather than a series of mechanisms which are solely or primarily 'done to us'.

Is 'corporate social responsibility' even possible? Some different positions

Interestingly, perspectives on whether it is even possible or desirable for cor-porations to be social responsible do not map as easily onto a political grid as might be expected. CSR breeds unlikely bedfellows, and so there are some odd connections between the opinions of the most anti-corporate of campaigners and the most right-wing of free-market, pro-corporate business economists.

Milton Friedman, for example, the Nobel Prize-winning economist who advocated the minimization of the state and increased power to corporations, argued that what he termed 'the new moralism' in business is in fact immoral. There is but one 'social responsibility' for corporate executives, Freidman believed: they must make as much profit as possible for their shareholders. This is their moral imperative. Executives who choose social and environ-mental goals over profits are, on the contrary, following muddled thinking, meddling with 'externalities' and producing a 'fundamentally subversive doctrine' that interferes with the free rein of market forces.

Friedman, a profoundly right-wing economist whose theories of *laissez-faire* capitalism were extremely influential on Western conservative thought during the final quarter of the twentieth century, therefore believed that corporations trying to practise 'social responsibility' were, in effect, putting into play a harmful scam. As he put it:

Of course, in practice the doctrine of social responsibility is frequently a cloak for actions that are justified on other grounds rather than a reason for those actions ... Whether blameworthy or not, the use of the cloak of social responsibility, and the nonsense spoken in its name by influential and prestigious businessmen, does clearly harm the foundations of a free society.

(Friedman 1970)

Friedman was already writing about corporations practising 'social responsibility' long before the term 'corporate social responsibility' emerged in the 1990s, to take on a life of its own (as I discuss more fully below). But the points he makes remain one of the clearest expressions of a right-wing, pro-free market stance, a stance which views the idea of corporations being 'responsible' for anything other than generating profit for their shareholders with profound scepticism. His words simultaneously endorse a very raw form of capitalism and perform a fairly graphic expression of capitalism's relationship to the social (in this sense, they at least have a refreshing clarity to them).

Friedman's position might be summarized as 'pro-corporate and anti-CSR'. It is a position shared by such latter-day Friedmanites such as Steve Forbes, the editor of *Forbes* magazine, and business academic David Henderson, who wrote a book lambasting CSR as a *Misguided Virtue* (see Henderson 2001, 2004). But obviously not all right-wing economists/business men and women who wish to expand the powers of corporations are *against* the idea of corporate social responsibility. A second position – one we might (again somewhat crudely) label as 'pro-corporate and pro-CSR' – is perhaps currently the most prominent position in the matrix I am sketching here, given how many businesses and organizations have come to want to present themselves as socially responsible. We can see its presence in the plethora of business books published on the subject, amidst business courses devoted to discussing its permutations, via business lobby groups which try to encourage its practice, and through corporate social responsibility reports (and the advertising and media coverage which accompany them).[3] One example of this pro-corporate, pro-CSR position which presents CSR as a win–win scenario for company and society is the Kotler and Lee quote with which I opened this chapter – and indeed the title of their book encapsulates much of the spirit of this discourse: *Corporate Social Responsibility: Doing the Most Good for Your Company and Your Cause.*

The logic of pro-corporate, pro-CSR arguments can vary from an expression that generating profit should involve 'giving something back' to society (which is, interestingly, an expression that incorporates within it some seed of the sense of having *taken something away*, though this is of course rarely if ever stated) right through to a more fully-fledged argument that businesses or corporations are the most effective guardians or agents of social care. In the latter vein, for example, Michael Hopkins' recent book *Corporate Social Responsibility and International Development: Is Business the Solution?* answers its own question with a resounding 'yes' (Hopkins 2007). As part of such narratives, CSR is often placed in a longer (and recently invented) historical tradition relationship between business and social care: for example, at a debate at London's ICA on CSR, John Williams, a member of two UK business groups championing CSR – Tomorrow's Company and Business in the Community – cited the 'social engineering' of the Merseyside village, Port Sunlight (built from the profits of Sunlight soap for the workers of Lever Bros) as part of CSR's heritage.[4] For this pro-corporate, pro-CSR stance, the question that there might be anything structurally or systemically wrong at all with corporate capitalism rarely features to any significant extent. Crucially, for this discourse to work, corporations have to be understood as socially and politically 'neutral' institutions.

Against this lies its polar opposite: the anti-corporate, anti-CSR stance. This discourse is vividly represented by the 2004 Canadian documentary *The Corporation,* and accompanying book written by Joel Bakan (who also wrote the film's script). The documentary traces the story of the American corporation from its earliest emergence in the eighteenth century as a public company that was legally positioned as subordinate to the public good. It presents the moment after the American Civil War as a rupture in this story when the Fourteenth Amendment – passed to help ensure the rights of former slaves by ensuring 'equal protection for all persons' – was seized upon by corporations who claimed that their rights had also been damaged and campaigned for damages to their corporate 'person'; between 1890 and 1910, out of the 307 cases brought to the Supreme Court using this amendment, 19 were brought by African Americans, 288 by corporations. From this moment, the rights of a corporation became equivalent to the rights of a person, and the film's central conceit is to pose the question: if the corporation is a person, what kind of person is it? To which its answer is: a psychopath (Abbott and Ackbar 2003; Bakan 2004).

Corporate social responsibility, in the version represented by *The Corporation,* is a scam, a deception by the sociopathic corporation. Discussing British Petroleum (BP), one of the most prominent and award-winning of CSR players with the most highly publicized forays into socially responsibility, having rebranded itself as 'beyond petroleum' (its adverts ask 'Can business be about more than profits?' and answer 'We think so'), Bakan points out that such initiatives can only be pursued insofar as they do not contradict the corporation's bottom line – which is to pursue profit for its shareholders. He contrasts BP's trumpeting of its environmental credentials with their recent expansion of oil drilling on the Alaskan coastal plain near Prudhoe Bay, discussing how it involves the displacement of Yukon people, the caribou herds (on which they depend for survival) being destroyed, and environmental devastation to Arctic ice (Bakan 2004: 35–46). Bakan argues that BP's aim is to continue to maintain demand for petrochemicals while they remain the key source of profit. CSR here, then, is a tautology: it is structurally impossible as corporations have shareholder profit rather than social good as their fundamental driver. It is over this specific point that such anti-corporate perspectives correlate with *pro*-corporate perspectives such as Milton Friedman's. (Indeed, Bakan features Friedman in the film, made shortly before Friedman died in 2006.) Similar anti-corporate, anti-CSR stances are expressed by the UK-based anti-corporate 'watchdog' magazine *Corporate Watch* and the popular American book *Toxic Sludge is Good For You* (Stauber and Rampton 1995).

But what of the remaining position in this quartet of stances I am sketching out: the anti-corporate, pro-CSR position? Unsurprisingly, this is in some ways the least habitable of positions. The closest to it is taken by lobby groups and NGOS which, like Bakan and Friedman, work on the assumption that corporations act to prioritize the bottom line to their shareholders. Like Bakan and Friedman, they also argue that CSR is not therefore an effective route through which to tend society; but they move away from this position by arguing that the law over corporate social responsibility and corporate behaviour therefore needs to be changed. In the UK, for instance, the lobby group the CORE coalition – primarily comprising of over 130 charities and campaigning organizations (including Amnesty International UK, War on Want and the World Wildlife Fund) and supported by a number of unions, MPs and co-operative businesses – have campaigned to reform the laws over corporate social responsibility. Broadly, the coalition have argued that the 'voluntary' approach towards CSR is ineffective and have campaigned for corporations to produce mandatory social reporting and for these CSR reports to follow much more stringent guidelines.[5]

However, CORE ('the corporate responsibility coalition'), like the many NGOs who belong to it, and who have published their own reports on CSR (such as Christian Aid) would never explicitly describe themselves as 'anti-corporate': their strategy is to reform business, and this involves using a vocabulary that does not alienate constituencies they wish to persuade, even though their membership obviously does not include many corporations. As Christian Aid puts it, 'Christian Aid, of course, supports responsible and ethical action by business', before detailing how the charity's experience of engaging with businesses such as British American Tobacco (BAT) led to the corporation publicizing their meetings to promote its CSR profile while failing to deal with their concerns (Christian Aid 2004: 42–3). Moreover, such groups can often at times inhabit a more wholly oppositional stance towards CSR itself: the 2007 Save the Children UK/ CORE report, *Why Corporate Social Responsibility is Failing Children*, for instance, argues that 'corporate social responsibility' should be replaced with 'corporate social *accountability*', to shift the emphasis onto *scrutinizing* corporate behaviour and away from any assumption that corporations can regulate themselves. 'Corporate social responsibility', they argue, cedes too much to corporations as entities by implying that they *should* have power over the social (Save the Children and the CORE Coalition 2007). Or as one of the most articulate media commentators on CSR, CORE spokesperson Deborah Doane, puts it elsewhere, 'Let's not put business in charge of the global commons, as the social responsibility agenda intends to do. That is the role of governments' (Doane 2003b). Whether we agree with Doane's assessment that it is the role of government to be 'in charge of the global commons' or not, the point of this argument is clear: CSR is here read as a way for corporations to control more and more aspects of social life and public provision.

The existence of CORE and NGO reports like *Behind the Mask* and *Why Corporate Social Responsibility is Failing Children,* then, points to a body of opinion that problematizes the categorical distinctions I have laid out, as they slide between being pro- and anti-corporate and pro- and anti-CSR. It is worth pointing out that all the examples in my categories might be complicated a little: Bakan, for example, also argues for legal reform, and in this sense is not so simplistically 'anti'-CSR; and some groups in the 'pro-corporate, pro-CSR' stance have violently different opinions over what CSR should entail. But it is this latter, large category, into which the work of many NGOs falls, which troubles the categorizations the most. In itself, this is indicative of the problems faced by or posed by the current position and power of NGOs, which have, as we saw in the previous chapter, large symbolic public lobbying power (Harvey 2005: 177–9; Beck 2006: 93) and, as such, scope to critique both governments and corporations; and around which anxieties are simultaneously circulating around the extent to which they become beholden to agendas outside of themselves – whether governmental or corporate – whether through funding or in an attempt to shape agendas. To some extent, they represent one of the most pivotal faultlines through which the whole problematic of tensions in this area can be thought.[6]

It could perhaps be said that because of these tensions the fourth 'anti-corporate, pro-CSR position' breaks down and is an unsustainable category. But perhaps what we actually see happening here is the political paralysis NGOs can face by oscillating between these positions. Their position often logically gestures towards occupying an anti-corporate stance, but they are frequently afraid of developing their practice to that conclusion for political reasons. In these terms, their oscillation is symptomatic of the problems of 'reformism'. The existence of these issues indicate how the categories I have been using in this section need to be expanded upon, and so at this point I want to turn to a different explanatory framework, later to be connected back to this one, to 'explain' CSR: the history of corporate philanthropy and the rise of the post-Fordist promotional/information society. For CSR, I suggest, can be understood as a paradigmatically post-Fordist form of corporate promotion as well as mode of corporate philanthropy. The next section explores the fusion between these areas.

CSR as post-Fordist promotional philanthropy

> Attitudes have changed. All of us have woken up to the global impact we can make.
>
> (John Williams, chair, *Tomorrow's Company* (ICA 2004))

As we saw in the previous section, CSR champion John Williams suggested that CSR had precursors in earlier forms of corporate social provision such as Lever Bros' building of the model village Port Sunlight in north-west England at the turn of the twentieth century from the profits of Sunlight soap. Williams is not alone in positing what we might term a 'long history' for CSR: many business books on the subject, in particular, open by suggesting and inventing some kind of tradition for it, citing extended histories of corporate 'giving' (see, for example, Hopkins 2003: 1). However, I suggest that it might be less useful to prematurely take these traditions for granted as some kind of 'historical truth' and more useful to think about these histories contextually and critically. Theories of the rise of post-Fordist information society and its associated forms of media promotion might be mobilized as a particular lens through which to view histories of corporate 'benevolence'.

Histories of corporate activity 'for the social good' might be split into two separate yet overlapping areas: corporate welfare and corporate philanthropy. Corporate philanthropy involves acts of often ostentatious giving by corporations to 'good causes', whether relief for the poor or the establishment of cultural institutions. There is a relatively large body of work interrogating how such corporate endowments have acted as mechanisms through which corporations have attempted to cleanse themselves of problematic histories of exploitation and enshrine themselves (and/or their founder) in public memory (Clifford 1988; Smith 1994a, 1994b; Duncan 1995; Wu 2002). Carol Duncan's work, for instance, on the 'civilising rituals' of art galleries and museums, outlines how business leaders rid themselves and their company of unsavoury connotations (such as slavery and worker exploitation), channelling the fortunes acquired on the backs of other people's labour into memorials for themselves, and refashioning their image into that of caring philanthropists providing services for the community, in the process (Duncan 1995: 72–101). Anglo-American culture is littered with such examples of corporate benevolence (the Tate Gallery, built on slavery and a sugar empire, being one good example). Such corporate philanthropy – at its zenith in the *laissez-faire* economic climate of the nineteenth century – has, importantly, been historically distinct from CSR in that the process has mainly worked by the object of its munificence being *outside* of or very distanced from 'the business of its business'. This is a fundamental and important part of the mechanism through which the company image is 'cleansed'.

The other strand of this history is corporate welfare. This has mainly entailed corporations and businesses providing welfare-related support for their workers. Into this category fall the particularly graphic examples of a number of mid- to late-nineteenth-century 'model villages': Port Sunlight, built, as we have seen, in Merseyside for Lever Bros' soap workers; Bournville, the housing complex built in Birmingham by Cadbury; or Saltaire, the town in Bradford built by Sir Titus Salt for his textile workers. Such forms of corporate 'responsibility' operated, by and large, in an opposite direction to the cleansing-via-*distance* mechanism of philanthropy mentioned above. By contrast, corporate welfare was entrenched in the corporate backyard (or 'home') through attempts to improve and regulate the material conditions of workers. Such initiatives, interestingly, span the political spectrum. They range from the Scottish village 'New Lanark', founded by Robert Owen and organized along co-operative principles, to liberal capitalist-welfare enterprises such as the London Brick Company's workers' village in England, 'Stewartby' (and include some villages whose organization uncomfortably resembles that of slave colonies). What unites these politically disparate models of corporate welfare, however, is their *paternalism*.

Such paternalism was adopted by car manufacturer Henry Ford, who in the 1910s began a fairly expansive system of corporate welfare which involved raising his employees' wages, shortening the working day and regulating his workers' off-duty social and sexual conduct (Bakan 2004: 35–6; Wyatt 2005). Ford's system is particularly significant because it became paradigmatic of a broader social and economic epoch, one that its name was also used to define: Fordism. 'Fordism' came to indicate both a system of hierarchical, standardized mass production that churned out vast numbers of goods through repetitive manufacturing (Gramsci 1934/1988; Harvey 1989: 125–40) and the broader contours of an 'era' in the middle decades of the twentieth century (Murray 1989: 38–53; Lee 1993: 71–9). Crucially, Fordism was marked by the continuation of a social system that entailed a crude segmentation by class, that involved white and male-dominated hierarchies, and that co-existed with the introduction of social democratic welfare programmes – which included, in the UK, the formation of the Welfare State, and in the USA, the work of FDR's 'New Deal'. These systems, which sought to curb the worst excesses of liberal capitalism by introducing social and economic safety nets – in the form of, for example, universal education and pensions, and in the UK, free public healthcare – can be thought of as a larger abstraction of the Fordist system of 'capitalist welfarism'. For one of the most frequently cited tropes of Ford's system is that Ford treated his workers much better because he realized they were also going to be his consumers: that Fordism therefore enshrined a new system in which *the worker was also the consumer* (Murray 1989: 41; Lee 1993: 79–80; Goldblatt 2000: 130). This can be extrapolated more broadly in terms of how it is mirrored by the settlement of Fordism as a Western social, cultural and economic system. A key plank of post-war Keynesian economics, for example, was guided by the logic of providing citizens with enough money to spend on its products (Hennessey 2006: 6–62).

In relation to these contexts, a case can be made for CSR as a paradigmatic invention of a post-Fordist information society which nonetheless draws on both the ethics of Fordism and returns to an earlier, nineteenth-century imagining of the relative positions of worker and consumer. It is distinct from (and yet related to) social 'responsibility' as characterized by either the creation of: (1) a cleansing distance from corporate behaviour (as with corporate philanthropy) or (2) a direct paternalism towards worker-consumers who are imagined, under Fordism, as more or less the same constituency. For the advent of corporate social responsibility involves a philanthropic system which is not so 'distanced' from the business of business but rather *integrated* into it. And it is a system that involves a significant shift from the Fordist model of corporate welfare, as consumers of goods are now imagined to be predominantly separate from their initial producers. In this way, it is similar to a *pre-Fordist*, nineteenth-century model where consumers and producers were much more separate entities (which itself indicates one correlation between 'old' liberalism and neoliberalism). Now, however, there are different global geographies at play: and a key plank of corporate welfare is to persuade a geographically separate body of consumers of the soundness of a distant production process.

We can spot these patterns if we look at narratives about CSR's emergence, the vast majority of which situate it as a phenomenon emerging in the 1990s. Most business textbooks and articles discuss CSR as a practice that has involved a shift to integrating business goals more thoroughly with philanthropy. Craig Smith's (1994a) business article on CSR as 'The New Corporate Philanthropy', cited by marketing guru Philip Kotler as 'seminal', for example, summarizes CSR as 'a new strategic approach' of 'making long-term commitments to specific social issues and initiatives ... in a way that also advances business goals' (Smith 1994a). (Or, as Kotler more baldly glosses it, CSR '*does good* for the brand and the bottom line as well as the community') (Kotler and Lee 2006: 9). That such shifts work to narrow the distance between the promotional object of philanthropy and the 'business of the business' is also reflected in the examples given in these business and marketing textbooks. No self-respecting account of CSR, for example, fails to cite the way Shell dealt with its corporate behaviour and PR crisis over its environmental and human rights record in the mid-1990s, when Shell decided to sink the Brent Spar oil platform into the Atlantic and the Nigerian military government executed Ken Saro-Wiwa, a vociferous campaigner against Shell's policies in Nigeria. Shell's response – hiring one of the largest global PR firms (Shandwick), vastly expanding its in-house PR staff, seeking to 'dialogue' with NGOs who critiqued its practices, launching 'community development' initiatives, and creating in 1997 its *Statement of Business Principles,* has become literally a textbook case in CSR practice (Klein 2000: 386; Christian Aid 2004; de Jong *et al.* 2005: 110–24).

Whether it actually resulted in significant change, or just a 'shallow' response which resulted in few community benefits and instead worked to perpetuate exploitation by acting as a 'pay-off for access to land' in the Niger Delta (Christian Aid 2004: 26) and primarily 'tossing around trendy management terms [while] the old Shell remains' (Klein 2000: 386) is in these terms another matter (although one we will revisit later). The point here is that as an example it marks how CSR is both a continuation and a departure from earlier models of corporate welfare and corporate philanthropy. The corporation's 'philanthropy' became integrated with its long-term business objectives and sites of production, rather than being created through a separate sphere, such as art; and its corporate 'welfare' acted to persuade *consumers and investors* that the company's *producers and production environment* were being looked after – two groups which were now, to all intents and purposes, quite separate (rather than, as with Fordist welfare, more or less in the same place).

I will elaborate further in the next section on CSR's relationships with these new formations of workers. But first I want to note that such an 'integration' of philanthropy with the business of business, combined with the appeal to *consumers* over the welfare of *producers* (or 'the production context') perfectly fuses with another archetypically post-Fordist practice: the use of 'deep', emotionally oriented promotional strategies.[7] Extensive branding around 'emotional selling points', expressed through multiple sites and spaces, is a typically contemporary post-Fordist practice – and very different from the produce-now, market-later patterns of Fordism, when 'unique selling points' were promoted through a limited range of demarcated advertising channels (Slater 1997: 174; Moor 2007). The capacity of emotional selling points to affect deeply and through a variety of channels (or what marketers call 'through the line advertising') can, if done effectively, be both a cheaper and more pervasive form of promotional power. CSR is symptomatic of this approach. In the rise of CSR in the 1990s, for example, business scholar Craig Smith describes how AT&T's adoption of CSR revamped its image at little cost, effectively working as a form of 'integrated marketing' with 'results so successful in enhancing the company's image as an innovator that AT&T has been able to rely less on advertising campaigns' (Smith 1994a). Or, as *PR Week* emphasizes, to conduct CSR effectively, companies can show journalists that they have an integrated approach to CSR by offering them salient nuggets from case studies and examples of CSR practice that they can 'touch and feel' (Hansley 2005).

CSR's role as an affectively-oriented promotional strategy targeted at the consumer and investor can be seen to be of a piece with wider tendencies in post-Fordist promotional culture that aim to build 'brand confidence'. As the need for confidence implies, public anxiety about the reliability of brands is a pressing issue, and CSR is quite clearly also a means for corporations to address such 'brand anxiety' by attempting to manage the reputation to circumvent problems in a global information age.[8] For if new fast media technologies were used together with the globalized outsourcing of production (i.e. cheap labour in overseas factories) by corporations since the 1970s as a means to break through what was for them the 'constraints' of the Fordist Deal, the same new, fast media technologies simultaneously threaten to expose its effects. In terms of technological capacity, for example, it is easier than ever before for protestors or media crews to film or record images of sweatshop conditions of production and for such images to reach a relatively wide audience of potential consumers (see Ross 1997; de Jong *et al.* 2005). In these terms the media management of corporate reputation simply matters much more: both because labour practices have become more violently removed from older (nationalistic) norms of corporate welfare, and because such production contexts and their effects have the possibility of becoming more graphically *visible*.

CSR therefore offers a form of reputation management in the face of criticism: it offers a damage limitation or risk avoidance strategy. As Jim McGuigan puts it, 'Public understanding and political struggles over risk are hugely dependent on their articulation by modern media of communication' (2006b: 215). As corporations both generate and attempt to manage risk, CSR discourse clearly becomes a key weapon in the corporate arsenal against 'personal' risk to itself (on this culture of risk more broadly, see Beck 1994).[9] For it is notable that it is primarily the most controversial and wealthy companies who 'excel' at CSR. The way their profit is made comes under fire, and so it becomes profitable for them to rebuild their image. In this sense, CSR might be thought of as the PR equivalent of a carbon offset. Shell, as we have already seen, is widely credited with launching the trend for modern CSR after its PR scares. Bernard Matthews, the UK poultry farmer synonymous with intensive factory farming and bird flu food panics, has won a UK CSR award.[10] British American Tobacco (BAT) and the arms dealer BAE have both won awards for their CSR programmes (and it could be pointed out that such award systems serve to validate the whole area further). All these companies clearly have controversial products, which has led critics to argue that 'social responsibility' cannot stretch very far. The idea that tobacco and arms manufacturing make the world a safer place, for example, argues Doane, pointing out how BAE's CSR award was for the reduction of its harmful paint on guns, 'isn't just silly: it's absurd' (Doane 2004: 82). In addition to the nature of the business being controversial, both continue to be lambasted by NGOs for their labour practices – BAT, for instance, for encouraging its Kenyan suppliers to work with grossly toxic pesticides which it sells to them direct (Christian Aid 2004: 34–43). Indeed, BAT is now included on the Dow Jones Sustainability Index (leading a New Economics Foundation report to argue that 'when dealing with long term issues of survival ... the Dow Jones Index is closer to being an "Unsustainability Index"') (New Economics Foundation 2002: 10).

While the need to cope with increasingly fast-paced global media and information flows partly explain how and why corporations respond to, or pre-empt, bad PR through CSR programmes to reassure their consumers and investors, they simultaneously point to the *unequal* concentrations of such global information (see Couldry and Curran 2003) which undermine consumers' abilities to make 'free choices'. It is much easier for a large corporation to obtain widespread access to media power. How familiar are most consumers, for example, with the detail of corporate exploitation? While BP's strapline 'beyond petroleum' and leaf-logo is now very familiar, how widespread and familiar are the details of its controversial behaviour in the Yukon? How many Western/Northern consumers could name the Etegwe, the part of Bayelsea in the Niger Delta where Shell dumped oil?

Harnessing desire, capitalizing on conscience: channelling social change

> Businesses, most of all, are run by people. They are societies of people, just like you, just like me. And I do not believe that all the nice people join Christian Aid and all the nasty people join corporations.
>
> (Mallen Baker, ICA debate on CSR, London 2004)

In *Cold Intimacies: The Making of Emotional Capitalism*, cultural sociologist Eva Illouz highlights how the trope of 'communication' has slowly become positioned at the forefront of contemporary life, from the foregrounding of the puzzle of emotional problem-solving in relationships to how, in a corporate universe 'saturated with affect', communication is a prized skill (2007: 23). Illouz is describing the process by which

> [t]he therapeutic idea of 'communication' came to designate the emotional, linguistic and ultimately personal attributes required to be a good manager and a competent member of a corporation. The

notion of 'communication' – and of what I would almost like to call 'communicative competence' – is an outstanding example of what Foucault called an episteme, a new object of knowledge which in turn generates new instruments and practices of knowledge.

(Illouz 2007: 18)

Illouz's book is concerned with the various ways these models of communication have become abstracted and rationalized: on-line dating services offer new technologies of interaction but are coldly rational; business discourse realigns emotional awareness and communicability into something to put on your CV. The book's argument can be related to broader accounts of the cultural turn (Hall 1997: 208–38; du Gay and Pryke 2002) but Illouz's suggestion that the contemporary fuss around communication has turned into a new episteme is very interesting in this context, given that CSR practices are closely tied to and frequently surface out of departments of 'corporate communications'. For the growth of 'corporate communications' vividly illustrates Illouz's argument that 'communication has come to define the model of corporate selfhood' (2007: 22). In addition, it indicates the contemporary prioritization of marketing to the vast majority of organizations and, in broader terms, a collapsed/converged promotional field in which, for example, PR is not so split off from advertising as it once was (Brierley 2002; Lury 2004).

The remit of corporate communications – that simultaneously important-sounding, and blandly generic term – includes CSR; and indeed, as we have seen, CSR discourse is a shining example of how 'external' communication, especially media management, is important for corporations. But corporate communications is also, as a thousand business courses demonstrate, concerned with the *internal* communicative workings of organizations (for a history, see Rose 1989: 81–119), and in this respect it is salutary to consider the affective and emotional role of corporate workers in the elaboration of CSR. By 'workers' here I am referring to what used to be called 'white-collar workers' (now a somewhat nostalgic-sounding term, gesturing to those pre-dress-down days before the white collar became less mandatory in Western/Northern office spaces).

For a little-remarked fact about CSR is that it often acts as a means to channel its employees' desires to facilitate 'progressive social change'. It mobilizes the emotional investments of its employees, the desire to 'do something extra', to break the corporate mould and 'act for the better'. BP, for example, uses CSR as a means of recruitment and to motivate its workforce, answering the question 'why work for BP?' by arguing at some length that 'the idea of being a "force for good" underlines all our activities worldwide ... the way we work is guided by values – integrity, honest dealing, treating everyone with respect and dignity, striving for mutual advantage'.[11]

Kotler cites 'increased ability to attract, motivate and retain employees' as a key reason for corporations to engage in CSR, highlighting the extra motivation that CSR can provide for morale-building in the workplace (Kotler and Lee 2006: 16). In an extension of this principle, the existence of Ronald McDonald House Charities, a core component of McDonald's CSR strategy providing aid for sick children and involving the vast majority of its branches, works to 'prevent the tensions that would otherwise develop between corporate HQ, franchises and suppliers' (Smith 1994a). CSR, in these terms, can function as a type of immaterial labour (Hardt and Negri 2005: 65) which utilizes aspects of an organization's internal communication: aspects which have traditionally been less prominent, or segmented within the realm of HR, but which are starting to receive more attention as a *resource* in the time of what Illouz terms 'the new communicative episteme'.

Most people want to work in companies that are *not* socially destructive. Such desire becomes more pronounced as media discussion of corporate exploitation – however minimal – grows. This is reflected in business discourse. As Kotler argues, even business graduates are increasingly looking for more meaningful and less exploitative work, citing a recent study showing that over half of MBA graduates 'would accept a lower salary in order to work for a socially responsible company' (Kotler and Lee 2006: 16). The performance of CSR can in these terms be a recruiting tool. One key question therefore might be whether the companies that workers believe to be socially responsible are actually worthy of that title to any significant degree, and what types of subjectivity – and forms of employee cynicism, denial, acceptance or negotiation – are played out in these contexts. Yet beyond, or besides, this question, the larger point it highlights is the 'incitement to discourse' around ethics and corporations. The noise, the interest, the investments around the subject are an entity that can be pushed and pulled in different directions. It is a live and active resource that can be mobilized for different cultural and political ends.

In these terms CSR appeals to workers' *desire* for democratic and participative cultures. It activates it. How this energy is *used* or oriented, by contrast, becomes a different matter. A useful point of comparison here is with work done in media studies by Mark Andrejevic and, in digital theory, by Tiziana Terranova on media participation. Both discuss how the promise of participative democracy in production is re-diverted by corporate producers. Andrejevic argues that viewer/consumer participation in reality TV programmes comes to offer 'a somewhat different and more cynical version of democratization' in which they are 'invited to sell their personal lives like labour power'; in which 'the participation of consumers in the rationalization of their own consumption is sold as empowerment' (2004: 6, 15). Terranova examines how corporations seek to 'harness' the creative democratic energies of people's interest and engagement in web and network cultures, transmuting it into 'free labour' (Terranova 2000, 2004). These techniques, which we might think of as 'participatory capitalism', have been variously described as 'post-post-Fordism', or 'prosumption' (Thrift 2006; Murray 2007).[12] There is therefore a parallel here with how corporations *draw on* their workers' desires to work in ethically responsible companies as a resource to bolster corporate profile and profits and as a means to manage their own risk.

This point, brought together with my earlier discussion of corporate welfare, enables us to gain a different perspective on the workings of CSR. In the context of the contemporary information society and promotional culture, where the possibility of media divulgence of corporate scandal may threaten shareholders (and, to a lesser extent, consumers), corporations can use CSR as a means to carry out corporate welfare, but in a different way than in the past. In other words, with CSR, corporations are looking after white-collar workers' *consumer concern* rather than their personal welfare: this concern and desire to do good form a resource, one which becomes oriented to solidify the corporation's ethical image and stakeholder value.

One reason why Andrejevic's and Terranova's models are so suggestive is because they move away from crude manipulation models and languages of 'truth' and 'falsehood' to instead focus on how flows of democratic energies become oriented within neoliberalism. They highlight the potential of producer and consumer energies, which both emphasizes the live mutability of these social and cultural relations, and opens up a sense of possibility which is crucial for any strands of optimism we might want or need to cultivate. This is a crucial factor here because, as we have seen, CSR as a discourse fundamentally plays on people's desires to do good – both as workers and consumers – and this is a factor which can be sidelined in some strains of anti-corporate discussion. As Mallen Baker puts it, in an implicit rejoinder to the sidelining of such discourse, 'I do not believe that all the nice people join Christian Aid and all the nasty people join corporations' (ICA 2004). To take this point to one extreme – indeed, to stretch it to breaking point – it could even be pointed out that some CEOs 'really want' to be socially responsible. There has been a fair amount of discussion, for example, about the extent to which the CEO of BP, John Browne, has 'deep convictions' about the need for business to 'be more responsible' in relation to the environment. As Bakan points out, however, within the current structure of corporate regulation, 'regardless of how deep and sincere his personal commitment to the environment is, as a CEO, Browne must put his company and its shareholders' interests above all others' (Bakan 2004: 41–3). More pressingly, the wider and more significant point is that workers' desires to work in unexploitative areas is a factor shaping corporate need to be seen to be involved with CSR.

In this light, the place we need to turn is to that crucial, yet profoundly unglamorous subject: regulation. Taking Andrejevic's and Terranova's points with us, along with some interesting strands of work on the subject (Hall

1997), we might treat this subject less in terms of a top-down process of arbitrary power grids imposed from without, and more of a process in which we organize ourselves as a society. How are we, in other words, orienting these discourses and energies? Who has the most power in channelling and influencing them?

Re-orienting regulation; or, who's responsible for responsibility?

Even though, as we have seen, it has its precedents, there is a fair amount of agreement that the term 'corporate social responsibility' was brought into being in the early 1990s. Many NGOs in particular highlight how the birth of modern CSR coincides, not uncoincidentally, with a large push by corporations to increase their own power, and with governments passing laws to facilitate this process: a process which commentators such as David Harvey term 'neoliberalism' (Harvey 2005). For Christian Aid, for example:

> modern CSR was born during the 1992 Earth Summit in Rio de Janeiro, when UN-sponsored recommendations on regulation were rejected in favour of a manifesto for voluntary self-regulation put forward by a coalition of companies called the World Business Council for Sustainable Development.
>
> (Christian Aid 2004: 2)

In these terms, CSR is a means for companies to regulate themselves in order to avoid further regulation so as to grow more powerful. George Monbiot, for example, summarizes this argument in reference to environmental politics by stating that 'at the heart of CSR is the notion that companies can regulate their own behaviour':

> By hiring green specialists to advise them on better management practices, they hope to persuade governments and the public that there is no need for compulsory measures. The great thing about voluntary restraint is that you can opt into or out of it as you please. There are no mandatory inspections, there is no sustained pressure for implementation. As soon as it becomes burdensome, the commitment can be dropped.
>
> (Monbiot 2002)

Monbiot cites as an example how Tony Blair's public request for Britain's major companies to publish environmental reports by the end of 2001 managed to defuse some of the mounting public pressure for government action; but, as it remained voluntary, three-quarters actually failed to report – a far less publicized fact.

Parallels can be made here between CSR and other industry practices – for example, with the advertising industry, which also campaigns to govern itself and to avoid external regulation (Brierley 2002: 210–25). However, the discourse of 'corporate social responsibility' makes a much larger claim than that of the advertising industry as it entails a *direct* pronouncement that corporations should have responsibility for 'the social'. In these terms we might see CSR as enabling corporations to have a social role as social democracy and welfare states decline – or, from the other end of the spectrum, as a tool used by corporations to promote this process: as a means for corporations to actively push social democracy and the welfare state *into* decline and thus as contributing to neoliberalism. It is not insignificant that CSR emerges after the breaking of Fordism's dams and the gradual erosion of state-directed social democratic welfare institutions. CSR in this respect can be understood as another driver in the process of '[d]eregulation, privatization, and withdrawal of the state from many areas of social provision' (Harvey 2005: 3).

Yet alongside this it is perhaps more empowering to consider how this system is not something solely 'done to us', but rather one in which we exist in multiple ways and participate in creating. Or, in Foucauldian terms, if such forms of social governance work through working on citizens' subjectivities, then they simultaneously highlight the very changeability and instability of such systems (Foucault 1982: 221).

In this light, one interesting interpretation of CSR as it currently stands as a system is expressed by the American commentator Bill McKibben, which is worth quoting at length:

> Helping corporations do the right thing through regulation . . . is not exactly a new idea. It's more or less what we used to do, in the long period from Teddy Roosevelt and the trustbusters on to about the 1980s.
>
> One reason for the shift is the enormous political power of corporations, which they use almost exclusively to boost their own profits. But in a way, you can't blame them for that. The strange part is how little opposition the corporate agenda meets anymore—how many of us have accepted the ideological argument that as long as we leave commerce alone, it will somehow, magically, solve all our problems. We could compel Big Oil to take its windfall profits and build windmills; instead we stand quietly by, as if unfettered plunder were the obvious and necessary course.
>
> Explaining this mystery may bring us back to where we started. In the childlike enchantment we've lived under since the Reagan era, we've wanted very much to believe that someone else, some wavy-

haired CEO, would do the hard, adult work of problem-solving. In fact, corporations are the infants of our society—they know very little except how to grow (though they're very good at that), and they howl when you set limits. Socializing them is the work of politics. It's about time we took it up again.

(McKibben 2006)

McKibben's argument is helpful in enabling corporate behaviour to be re-thought as an entity, or series of entities, that it is possible for people to be in control of, rather that something which is controlling them. This chimes with the kind of liberating theoretical positions, from Foucault through to the contemporary media and cultural studies analyses of Andrejevic and Terra-nova, which emphasize the possibilities for change; and from an NGO/CSR campaigning perspective, it chimes with positions that suggest that CSR needs to be regulated. But it is also interesting in how it points towards a particular myth: towards the myth that the *paternalism* of the Fordist deal (represented by the Welfare State/the New Deal/Fordism itself) evaporated in post-Fordism. As McKibben's work indicates, alongside a wide range of other analyses of corporate behaviour in the post-Fordist era, this is simply not so. (For instance, it resonates with Benjamin Barber's analysis of contemporary consumer society as exploiting children and infantilizing adults; Barber 2007). In many ways, it seems more useful to consider how we have replaced one form of public-sector-oriented paternalism with another: that of free-market corporate-driven liberalism. This, we might say, is a more *disaggregated* form of paternalism: and one which has gained much of its power through its performance of being neutral and by creating an image of a market that is 'open' or 'free'.

Given these contexts, how, then, might we shift responsibility away from mainly being the preserve of paternalist corporations?[13] Such debates prompt the questions: who is responsible for responsibility? And: what combination of strategies might be able to re-orient desires for a mode of social responsibility that is not solely beholden to the logic of corporations' short-term profit?

It is beyond the scope of this chapter to formulate such strategies, given that the book's remit is obviously an analytical one. But there are a few tendencies we might extrapolate when thinking about how to answer these questions. In particular, this chapter has shown that in significant ways the territory CSR can occupy is far larger and more powerful than that to which the discourse of ethical consumption can lay claim, and to which it has many similarities, but surpasses in its ability to re-orient consumer and worker anxieties and investments in ethics into solutions that often benefit only the short-term profits of corporations. The argument for a shift from CSR to CSA (corporate social accountability) is one that enables the live interest in the subject of CSR to be pushed in a direction in which corporations are accountable *to* the social, rather than being responsible *for* it.

Some commentators think 'the solution' to the question of who should be in charge of responsibility and regulation lies with governments (recall Doane's earlier comment: 'Let's not put business in charge of the global commons, as the social responsibility agenda intends to do. That is the role of governments'). This is one mechanism – flawed yet still significant – that remains available. Another is international regulation: many NGOs, for instance, argue that the UN needs to intervene to stop companies applying different standards overseas than to their 'home' behaviour (Christian Aid 2004: 59). And at the same time there are other conversations happening now about how we regulate ourselves as a society: about the lack of interest in political representative democracy and the possibilities for alternative kinds of participatory democratic processes (Wainwright 2003; Critchley 2007). We might, for example, consider the kind of local participatory community forum activity represented by TELCO, a community group in East London that campaigned for HSBC to pay its cleaners a living wage (Jamoul 2006) or the grassroots transnational campaigns to raise living standards in Western corporations' clothing factories (Ross 1997, 2008) as other forms of move-ment towards a participatory politics of corporate accountability. Strategi-cally, together, such a combination of approaches – from the international, to the national, to the participatory – might offer the most wide-ranging means to allow us to rethink who is, and who needs to be, 'responsible for respon-sibility'. But of course, the subject of activism also brings with it its own problems, and it is this subject to which the next chapter now turns.

4   Interior economies

Anti-consumer activism and the limits of reflexivity

By bringing the global flows linking corporate brands with sweatshop labour into a new level of popular visibility, the success of Naomi Klein's best-selling book *No Logo* facilitated the high-profile publication of similar books critiquing corporate power and contemporary consumerism (Hertz 2001; Schlosser 2002) and was itself enabled by the broader context of the movements for global justice which the book in part documents (Shepard and Hayduk 2002; Notes from Nowhere 2003; Wainwright 2003; Mertes 2004). But, by contrast, while the study of consumer culture has expanded in a multitude of interdisciplinary directions over the past two decades (Featherstone 1991; Nava *et al.* 1997; Slater 1997; *Journal of Consumer Culture* 2001–) academic studies of anti-consumerist activism have been relatively sparse. They have tended to focus on *histories* of consumer activism, and the little study of *contemporary* anti-consumerism there is available can often be more celebratory than critically interrogative (see, for example, Bordwell 2002). However, celebrating the 'resistance' of anti-consumerism will not get us very far in critically exploring its significance as the binaries of 'dominant' and 'resistant' are extremely limited tools of analysis. A more useful route to grappling with the complexities of anti-consumerist discourse might therefore be to use and extend some of the tools offered to us by cultural studies to understand and engage with contemporary anti-consumerist activism. For cultural studies has a rich tradition of both engaged participation and an ability to dissect the complex connections being made by its objects of study, through, for example, its models of articulation and transformative practice (see Laclau and Mouffe 1985; Grossberg 1997: 355; Hall 1997).

This chapter pursues this aim in one particular direction: by thinking through how different types of anti-consumerist activism imagine change happening, and how they envisage their own roles in relation to broader contexts; or what I call the 'interior economies' of anti-consumerism activist discourse. To do this, I focus the discussion on four particular examples, all of which relate, in their different ways, to various strands of anti-consumerism:

Klein's *No Logo*, Anita Roddick's (2001) manual *Take it Personally*, the work of the activist organization Adbusters, and Bill Talen's book *What Should I Do if Reverend Billy is in my Store?* In considering how these works position themselves as contributing to social and cultural change, the chapter attempts to identify what these anti-consumerist discourses understand as 'activism' and their own role in relation to it; the 'type' or characteristics of the (anti-) consumers they imagine; what narratives are being produced about how change happens; and what the implied consequences are for consumption and production.

Another way of putting this is to say that this particular analysis investigates the various ways in which these activist narratives can be understood as 'reflexive', and that it considers the possibilities and limitations of their various forms of reflexivity. To extend this discussion in more detail, the later part of the chapter draws on the work of Scott Lash, Donna Haraway, Judith Butler and Bruno Latour to draw out in more detail what might be termed 'the reflexive horizons' of different forms of anti-consumerism. In particular, I use them to suggest that two different types of reflexivity might be identified at work in anti-consumerist discourse, as well as in cultural theory: first, a relatively narcissistic form of reflexivity which acts to shore up an essentialized anti-consumerist activist self; and second, an understanding of reflexivity as a more relational and dispersed process.

The aim of this chapter, then, is to both focus on some of the possibilities and limitations of current anti-consumerist arguments, and to think about how these alternative systems of consumption are imagined as being brought into being. To begin with, let us turn our attention to one of the more dramatic instances that jump-started a new wave of popular debate about the problems of consumption: Naomi Klein's *No Logo*. I am primarily discussing *No Logo* here not because it is 'representative' but because of its important and fascinating status as an international best-seller. Starting with *No Logo* offers useful ways to think about the strengths and limitations of the reflexivity of anti-consumerist activism: of what is being understood as an anti-consumerist activist, and how its own work is understood and is being positioned in relation to this broader field of activity.

Identifying a politics: Klein's *No Logo*

> Then we had an idea. Maybe if we banged together the heads of all these activists and reconfigured the fragmented forces of identity politics into a new, empowered movement, maybe we could start winning again.
>
> (Adbusters founder Kalle Lasn, quoted in his book, *Culture Jam: the Uncooling of America*, Eagle Brook, 1999: xii)

> There is an economy in the interior of a person. We need to find a
> new kind of vivid privacy.
> (Bill Talen, better known as 'Reverend Billy' from The Church of
> Stop Shopping, in his book *What Should I Do if Reverend Billy is
> in my Store?* The New Press, 2003: 83)

The rejection of, negotiation with or attempt to create a new form of 'identity
politics' have been a key feature of many contemporary anti-consumerist
texts and actions. For example, in her last book, *Take it Personally*, the political
entrepreneur Anita Roddick states, spinning around that old motif of second-
wave feminism, is personal: and so 'the future of the world depends on us all
taking it personally'. But to Naomi Klein, focusing on the personal, on
identity politics, has primarily been part of the problem:

> Many of the battles we fought were over issues of 'representation' – a
> loosely defined set of grievances mostly lodged against the media,
> the curriculum and the English language. From campus feminists
> arguing over 'representation' of women on the reading lists to gays
> wanting better 'representation' on television, to rap stars bragging
> about 'representing' the ghettos, to the question that ends in a riot in
> Spike Lee's 1989 film *Do the Right Thing* – 'why are there no brothers
> on the wall?' – ours was a politics of mirrors and metaphors.
> (Klein 2000: 107)

Her generation of university students, she argues in Chapter 5 of *No Logo*,
were 'media narcissists' who focused on identity politics and on changing
representations of gender, 'race' and sexuality, but left issues of social
inequality untouched. 'We were too busy analyzing the pictures being projected on the wall', she writes, 'to notice that the wall itself had been sold'
(Klein 2000: 124). The demands of these kinds of identity politics, in Klein's
narrative, were partially met but mainly co-opted by corporate marketers,
who absorbed the demands for equality of representation into their pursuit of
private capital to be shared by the few.

  This tale of the co-option of left identity politics is a familiar one. As well
as being told by Klein in *No Logo* and historicized by Thomas Frank in *The
Conquest of Cool*,[1] it is frequently dropped into conversation by academics
such as Paul Gilroy, who has talked of how corporations have 'filleted' progressive ideas (Frank 1997; Smith 2000: 21). As Sheila Rowbotham put it in
her cultural autobiography of the 1960s, 'ironically, openings created by
social movements were to present market opportunities', leaving 'our
hopes ... appropriated, our aspirations twisted' (Rowbotham 2000: xiv–xv).
Recently the trope of co-option has been contested by writers who highlight
the role of 1960s/1970s counterculture as *contributing* to thicker, more

complex versions of late capitalism and the shift to post-Fordism, and in doing so enables us to conceptualize such phenomena as involving more complex transmutations and articulations than the image of a simplistic 'takeover' can at times allow (Binkley 2003; Boltanski and Chiapello 2006).

No Logo's response to the perceived co-option of left identity politics is in part, as we see above, to argue that identity politics was not substantial or concerned with economic justice enough in the first place and as such should be dismissed. And yet, I would argue, this brings us to a contradiction, for it is precisely No Logo's ability to make connections between identity politics and social inequality, precisely its act of linking these personal anecdotes and comments on media representation to examples of the extremities of global labour injustice which has created much of its cultural resonance and power. Take, for example, the beginning of the book, where Klein sets the global outsourcing scene by describing the 'ghost of a garment district' in Toronto where she lives. Here, while 'old Portuguese men still push racks of dresses and coats down the sidewalk',

> [t]he real action ... is down the block amid the stacks of edible jewelry at Sugar Mountain, the retro candy mecca, open at 2 a.m. to service the late-night ironic cravings of the club kids. And a store downstairs continues to do a modest trade in bald naked manne-quins, though more often than not it's rented out as the surreal set for a film school project or the tragically hip backdrop of a television interview.
>
> (Klein 2000: xiii)

Rather than simply take Klein to task for invoking an essentialized 'real', we might learn from observing something of the pragmatics of its function. Here the 'real' of 'the real action' is not only what is perceived as quantitatively important, but as most qualitatively and experientially significant. In other words, what is being posited as being to some extent most initially socially pressing and culturally engaging (most 'real'), is the Generation X Northern/ Western youth from which Klein writes – and to a large extent, to which she writes. At the same time the narrative can demonstrate a reflexive awareness that it is addressing and privileging this particular constituency. As Klein's authorial persona shifts from downtown Toronto to a factory on the outskirts of Jakarta, where she interviews Indonesian factory workers (described as global 'roommates of sorts', connected through products and brands) she ruefully acknowledges how 'being the Western foreigner, I wanted to know what brand of garments they produced at the Kaho factory – if I was to bring their story home, I would have to have my journalistic hook' (Klein 2000: xv).

The book is presented as an exercise in defetishization, in connection-tracing, in linking the products of the contemporary life Klein shares with her assumed audience back to the stages of their production, and there is a degree of reflexivity about to whom, how and why the story is being told. But we can also see how the success of *No Logo*'s critique of brands is dependent on Klein's acute eye for the vagaries of Western, middle-class, Generation X consumer culture. It speaks primarily to those in such groups with similar broadly sketched cultures of taste and *habitus* (those who have bought Nike clothes, those who can remember designer label culture, those who have ever been interpellated by 'youth' media) and such capacious lifestyle groupings have an extensive reach. Judith Williamson, wondering why Klein was focusing on the Nikes and the Tommy Hilfigers rather than Intel and major banks, '[g]radually ... grasped that *No Logo* is, at heart, a sort of *Bildungsroman* – the story of young North America's disillusion with capitalism, and its outrage at discovering the iniquities which fuel its own lifestyle' (Williamson 2002: 211). Many of *No Logo*'s chapters open with Klein's anecdotes about her own past and present experience. She recalls, for example, the classroom tyrant who went around checking designer t-shirt labels were not fake; recounts selling brands in the clothes shop Esprit; and describes how she and her brother begged her wholemeal parents for fast food (Klein 2000: 27, 143–5). In this way it functions to make connections between the structures of feeling inhabited by her readership and the context of global socio-economic inequality and exploitation.

To understand more fully why this is important, we might borrow a suggestive phrase from Lawrence Grossberg (adapted from a phrase of Rebecca Goldstein's, and merged with ideas of Deleuze and Guattari) of *mattering maps*.[2] These 'define where and how one can and does invest, and where and how one is empowered, made into an agent' (Grossberg 1997: 368; Grossberg 1992: 82, 398). In other words, 'mattering maps' are a way of considering how we not only have cognitive connections with cultural formations, but *affective* investments in them, investments of emotion, and feeling (feelings which are often prepersonal and are not necessarily libidinal). *No Logo* works to sketch a 'mattering map' for citizen-consumers of Generation X who can recognize their own experience. The book's *mise-en-scène* features snapshots of Klein's past and present that range across a variety of emotional states including shame, desire, embarrassment and pride. Alongside its investigative journalism into new protest cultures and the material origins of trainers, alongside its political exhortations, then, it speaks of and to emotional investments recurrent for a wide North American/European young constituency. This gives the text an affective pull that many other works analysing commodity fetishism do not always have.

As such, *No Logo* demonstrates the importance of taking into account the complexities of consumer identity, affect and desire when discussing alternative systems of consumption (for a survey of the recent explosion of work on affect, see Gregg and Seigworth, forthcoming). This is particularly marked in the context of anti-consumerist discourse, which has, historically, often been characterized by its inability to acknowledge consumer desire, or to acknowledge it in anything other than reductive terms (Belk 2003; Galtz 2004).[3] Equally, however, *No Logo* also gestures towards a gamut of potential problems with the role of identity politics in popular anti-consumerist and global justice texts. For instance: might the focus on the interpellated individual consumer who is having their lifestyle connected to wider sites and frameworks of exploitation lead to an individualized consumer politics? Who exactly can have 'identity' in these discourses – who is allowed to say 'I', and who is included in the 'we'? And how do such specific mattering maps in turn map onto imagining wider social changes in systems and networks of consumption and production?

Anti-consumerist activism in *No Logo* is positioned as contributing to cultural change in both an explicit and implicit fashion. First, it works explicitly, through the anti-capitalist activism which the second half of the book is devoted to documenting. Klein's discussion of such activism works as a powerful corrective to conservative media reports dominating the subject, and one important reason for its success is that it also works to galvanize optimism (or 'resources of hope'). But at times, its coverage can also be presented in almost vanguardist fashion, in that descriptions of the protests and social movements taking place from Seattle onwards can be depicted as the leaders of an anti-consumer revolution whose expansion and victory are almost inevitable (see Ritzer 2002). Jonathan Dollimore has used the phrase 'wishful theory' to describe theory which forces itself to find what it wishes to see (2001: 37–45), and occasionally the sheer glorification of the protests might be thought of as a kind of variant on this (what we might call 'wishful journalism'), which can at times push beyond the boundaries of a usefully promotional performative-becoming.

But, second, activism works *implicitly*, through the function of the book itself. The implication is that readers have to find their own way to activism, and yet, for those outside activist circles, or uninvolved in the kind of educational spheres where such activism is examined, perhaps the possibilities of connecting are less clear. The act of reading *No Logo* is itself probably one of the most significant investments in 'the movement-of-movements' that many people will make. This brings us to one of the most important, overlooked and problematic points about *No Logo*: the great issue – unspoken of in the text and Klein's following book, *Fences and Windows* – of the role for books like *No Logo* in putting such debates on the agenda and turning them into ideas that will seem to be popular and feasible. In short, the issue of mainstreaming, of coalition-building and creating broad-based counter-hegemonies. In effect, to discuss this is to discuss *the role of the commodity of the book itself as a form of activism*. It is to focus on the role of the book as praxis, or on what Gerard Genette would term its epitext, the discourse which is generated around a book which works to give it meaning (Genette 1997). While *No Logo* has taken a fair amount of flak for being published by a subsidiary imprint of News Corporation (Flamingo is owned by HarperCollins which is owned by News Corporation), the argument for *why this mode of publication is in itself a useful politics* is that, by using these tools of the transnational corporations, it has a discursive reach, and a popularizing role, that would be denied to it if it had been published by a small independent publisher. *No Logo*'s marked and widespread success may well, ironically, have already had just as much if not more impact than the protests it documents. Yet this factor is one with a strange status in the book's account of how change happens. It is simultaneously acted out and erased.

This disjuncture directly relates to another: the fetishization of the brand as cause and root of the ills of contemporary capitalism in *No Logo* rather than but one component of 'the problem' of a globalized late capitalist system. Clearly, using the multinational brand as a way of critiquing neoliberalism has enormous strengths and is a useful trope around which to generate a broad range of affective alliances. Yet one of its problems is that, as Michael Hardt has pointed out, 'it still risks focusing too much on corporations and leading to a politics that is merely anti-corporate' (2002: 221–2). It can mean, for example, only attacking large corporations while ignoring government policies which foster their inequalities. Klein begins to address some of the ramifications of the limitations of brand-based politics in the penultimate chapter in *No Logo*, 'Beyond the Brand'. Here, for example, she points out that when one logo is campaigned against, even when being used tactically to illustrate broader issues, 'other companies are unquestionably let off the hook'; notes that 'anticorporate activism walks a precarious line between self-satisfied consumer rights and engaged political action', and argues that the 'challenges of a global labor market are too vast to be defined – or limited – by our interests as consumers' (Klein 2000: 428). Such gestures towards 'moving beyond' brand-based politics continue into her next book, *Fences and Windows*, which ends by stating that symbols such as brands 'were never the real targets; they were the levers, the handles. The symbols were only ever windows. It's time to move through them' (Klein 2002: 246).

This fetishization of brands as responsible for contemporary capitalism has a further effect, one which is particularly pertinent here, in that it can also enact a slippage between any form of promotional popularization and neoliberal branding. This leaves the fact that *No Logo* itself is clearly a logo (one used to popularize an anti-neoliberal project) only too painfully exposed to critique. In many ways, this fetishization of branding also has parallels to how advertising was 'scapegoated' as, almost by itself, responsible for capitalism in the 1970s and 1980s, the critique of which position in turn became the staple fare of academic studies of consumer culture in the 1990s (see Nava *et al.* 1997). One task therefore seems to be to consider how it is possible to use branding as a way into such debates without fetishizing it; to find languages to distinguish between its various modes, between the discourses to which 'the brand' in question – whether Nike Air, or *No Logo* – is articulated; for 'branding' can function as an empty signifier, or a screen on which to project various interests (see Arvidsson 2005; Moor 2007). In the terms in which I am particularly interested here – of thinking about *No Logo*'s reflexivity as an activist text – what this means is that there is a mismatch between its popular activist role and the explicit politics foregrounded in the book. There is a slippage between how 'branding' signifies neoliberal branding, the populist promotion of the book itself and its non-neoliberal alternatives. In short, *the role of popular anti-neoliberalism as promotional discourse is simultaneously acted out in praxis and denied at the level of discussion.*

No Logo therefore stages a rejection of identity politics while performing a reconciliation with and reworking of it. It emphasizes the role of activist enclaves and vanguards in broader political change, but its own success and implicit function, through its very accessibility and through offering a widely identifiable mattering map, render it more of a populist strategy for generating counter-hegemonic discourse. It castigates branding as the key cause of neoliberalism, yet itself demonstrates – through its own strategy as a populist text – a more sophisticated understanding of the political uses of promotion in socio-political discursive change. There is a disjunction, then, between a praxis which is very sharply attuned to the role of discourse in social and cultural change, and an explicit, foregrounded narrative which does not discuss this, focusing instead on relatively small enclaves of avant-garde activism. We might regard this as an example of performative rhetoric or of a text working through its own contradictions and strategies. But, at another level, it also undeniably indicates a lack of reflexivity about the role of the book as praxis and – despite how the function of the book itself contradicts this – a strain of Romanticism about the perceived purity of 'activism'.

Taking it (all?) personally

No Logo shows that connecting abstract or macro-analyses of consumption to particular structures of feeling or singularities can work well to connect and generate shared experiences and affective investments. But it also begs the question of whether some anti-consumerist calls-to-arms might actually recommend more *individualized* solutions than the modes of consumption they critique. For a potential threat of anti-consumerist identity politics is that it might degenerate into the quasi-pathology of consumer heroism or individualized forms of consumer activism, rather than emphasizing the relationships and connections between consumers and producers (and consumers and consumers).

One example of such a problematically individualistic ethic is the late Anita Roddick's book *Take it Personally: How Globalisation Affects You and How to Fight Back* (2001). This is an 'action guide for conscious consumers' featuring lists of resources, alongside the writings of global justice campaigners, NGO workers and journalists. The text predominantly interpellates the reader as a 'rational choice' consumer who, once equipped with enough information, will be able to challenge globalization from a personal perspective (Roddick 2001: 42–3). The personalized identity politics of this anti-consumerist text engenders an over-investment in individual agency, in which a series of mainly middle-class individuals are awarded the task of remoulding consumption. All the sections – which include topics such as 'Activism', 'People' and 'Environment' – feature personalized introductions by Roddick. These include narratives of her own growth as an agent-of-change, from hanging around in her mother's café (framed as the prototype for the Body Shop) to her rise as a philanthrophic CEO bearing touristic witness to the effects of globalization.

> I've held mutated babies genetically handicapped by toxic waste dumped in local streams. I've spied on illegal loggers in Sarawak. I've seen babies living near Mexican tobacco fields that were born without genitalia – and if anything made me take it personally, that did.
>
> (Roddick 2001: 7)

While Roddick's pronouncements do consider the relationships between producers and consumers in the North and South, and while Roddick herself had a history of contributing to a number of progressive/left causes (see Kalhar 2008) there are important limitations to her 'identity politics' in *Take it Personally*. In this example, for instance, the persistent focus on 'otherness' (and the innocent sanctity of childhood) is clearly problematic. It indicates little of the *complexities* of Northern consumer subjectivities that rely on these abuses for their lifestyle. The personal anecdotes are unproblematically self-congratulatory; compared to Klein, there is little sense of reflexivity about either her role or the emotional investments which matter to her. Because of this, Roddick's narrative of the corporate success story of a CEO who still identifies with 'the people' can easily slip into a rhetoric of patronage rather than egalitarian connection. Its self-aggrandizement enlarges the role of the individual, pushing it closer to the grandiose individualism of celebrity, rather than dissolving it into singularities of shared experience (Deleuze 1995: 6–7). Klein, in contrast, as we have seen, registers awareness of the dangers of slipping into a politics which degenerates 'into glorified ethical shopping guides: how-to's on saving the world through boycotts and personal lifestyle choices ... the challenges of a global labor market are too vast to be defined – or limited – by our interests as consumers' (Klein 2000: 428). In *Take it*

Personally, Roddick's strain of personal-growth terror-tourism, combined with the consumer-exoticism which is the Body Shop's stock-in-trade (Ware 1992: 243–8; Kaplan 1999: 139–56) can at times lend the title of the book an unintentionally ironic flavour.[4]

There are, however, also similarities with *No Logo*'s more extensive forms of reflexivity; as both books dramatize the historical genealogy of a particular ethics of the activist self, and narrating the reasons why they have come to formulate the relationship to their 'selves' that they have. In his discussion of 'The Cultivation of the Self' in the third volume of *The History of Sexuality* Foucault points out that complex processes of 'individualism' include 'the intensity of the relations to self, that is, of the forms in which one is called upon to take oneself as an object of knowledge and a field of action, so as to transform, correct, and purify oneself, and find salvation' (Foucault 1986: 42). *No Logo* can be read as a narrative in which Klein often takes herself as 'an object of knowledge and a field of action', dramatizing her own move towards an attempt to purify herself and 'find salvation'. But, with Klein, this latter stage is gestured towards as a *goal* to be reached: the text does not offer any codified account of *achieved* heroic anti-consumer salvation, unlike Roddick's narrative. Where perhaps less reflexivity is indicated in Klein's case is how the anti-consumerist *activist self* becomes an object of knowledge: or, in other words, how Klein is in a position to write in the first place (and this is also the case with *Take it Personally*).

While the 'movement-of-movements' is not predominantly 'white' in global terms, in Europe and North America, it has been known for featuring large amounts of white middle-class activists, although there are signs that this is changing. Bhumika Muchhala, active in the 'Students against sweat-shops' campaign in the USA, puts this very interestingly:

> As with the mobilizations at Seattle and elsewhere, it's predominantly a white movement. Though the conditions in sweatshops resonate with Latinos and the Asian diaspora, these people aren't yet as politically active on campuses – *perhaps because they don't feel comfortable in organizing culture.*
>
> (Muchhala 2004: 199; my emphasis)

In other words, for those who are low in different kinds of social or cultural capital, it can be hard enough to even get a foot onto the pitch, let alone attempt to reconfigure the rules of the game. The point of such an observation is not to attack *No Logo*, a text which often explicitly attempts to encourage multiple points of identification (placing, for example a high importance on the exploitation of 'black' cultures) but rather to help us understand how Klein, like Roddick, is able to be in the very position to write this book.

Unholy investments

While Roddick's identificatory investments are presented as being seamlessly unproblematic, and Klein's more complex investments are all presented as happening in the past, evocative mattering maps of anti-consumerist activists which assess the vagaries of their route to activism and the continuation of complexities in the present do exist. Bill Talen, for example, who becomes the persona 'Reverend Billy' of 'The Church of Stop Shopping', is more revealing of his activist investments in his book *What Should I Do if Reverend Billy is in my Store?* The preacher and his gospel-singing church are perhaps best known for their Situationist-inspired invasions of branches of Starbucks, in which they stage impromptu theatrics against the café chain's bullying of smaller traders, its exploitation of coffee growers, and the homogeneity of its consumer environments (see http://revbilly.com; Kingsnorth 2003). These activities have been recorded and dramatized in Rob VanAlkemade and Morgan Spurlock's documentary *What Would Jesus Buy?* (VanAlkemade 2007). Working as an ironic strategy which pre-empts accusations of puritanism, humourlessness and 'worthiness' because of its anti-consumerist ideological stance, and dramatizing the *oddness* of attempting *not* to participate so fully in corporate consumer culture (which '[o]fficially ... is absurd, an anti-gesture, like an American who didn't go west, who didn't go into space, who had sex without a car', Talen 2003: xiii), Reverend Billy's performances have included a range of similar street and shop activist-theatre events including anti-consumerist 'conversions', blessings on sidewalks and choreographed mobile phone actions in Disney stores. *What Should I Do if Reverend Billy is in my Store?* describes Talen's moments of being empowered, of finding agency, and of working with people, alongside moments of 'True Embarrassment' (of the 'embarrassing moment that is revelatory' Talen 2003: 66, 82) of disillusion, doubt and being 'exhausted by loneliness' (2003: 57).

If, in *No Logo*, Klein produces momentary reflexive accounts of her past relationship to consumerism, on the nature of alliances and ties to other consumers, so does Talen, but he also does something more. Talen's reflections about his investments are particularly interesting because so many texts around the global justice movement are ethnographic travelogues, stories which unproblematically celebrate anti-neoliberal activism without connecting this to the activities, lives and investments of those who do not have the time or cultural capital to be full-time activists, or without offering much reflexivity about the investments of the activist themselves (for critiques, see Soar 2000; Gilbert 2008). Talen's complex narratives about the different relationship of people in 'the church' to consumerism, and some of the variable reasons for his own investments *in the present* as well as in the past, therefore form something of a contrast with how Klein's and Roddick's attempts to keep their own activist-present relatively 'pure'.

But in some ways, while being layered with irony, Reverend Billy's narratives follow the tradition of positing psychological and material existence 'outside' of western consumer culture as 'the real', against which consumerism is merely a continuing shadow on the walls of Plato's cave (Bowlby 1993). Anti-consumerism is linked in a chain of equivalence to psychological completeness and to the rediscovery of an Edenic type of community which has been lost – what Reverend Billy calls 'ordinary life' and what Jean Luc-Nancy calls 'the phantasms of the lost community' (Talen 2003: xiv–xv; Nancy 1991: 12). And yet, there is at the same time an impetus to break from this discourse, to understand the important social and cultural bonds which can be forged from contemporary consumption (watching the shoppers, he writes 'they were locked in their dance together. Maybe theirs was a kind of community after all', Talen 2003: 56). There is also a sense of community which is defined not as a mythical 'wholeness' to be reconstituted, but rather, as in Nancy's sense, as resistance to immanent power. For instance, Talen writes of how the 'vivid privacy' which he thinks is necessary to find is ironically always accompanied by a community of support (Talen 2003: 83). In Reverend Billy's words and actions, then, interwoven through the irony, there is a concern to understand contemporary psychologies and socialities of consumption, to recognize 'the reach and grasp of desire that drives the purchase' (Talen 2003: 74). In other words, it demonstrates an interest in the psychologies of consumer and anti-consumer behaviour, and in how changes to such behaviour happens.

The performance of 'Reverend Billy' is therefore an oscillating fusion of the languages of discovering relatively essentialized 'real' pre-consumerist identities, and of the possibilities of creating, of *becoming* new forms of post-consumerist communal beings. 'There is an economy in the interior of a person', Talen writes, and we needed to 'find a new kind of vivid privacy' (Talen 2003: 83). This 'interior economy' is, simultaneously, a quasi-nostalgic defence of a private space, one which constitutes the 'real' pre-lapsarian consumer imaginary, and a strategic way of understanding the constructions, and the becomings, of new anti-consumerist activist subjectivities.

Reverend Billy and his Church epitomize anti-consumerism in one of its most entertainingly camp forms. They exemplify the politics of 'boycott culture', mixed prominently with a flamboyant advocation of consumer abstinence.[5] For some commentators, their approach simply works to ramify the publicity given to the brands in question, or runs the risk of stasis through its irony (Moore 2007: 48–52). But like the promoters of Buy Nothing Day, in which consumers are encouraged not to buy anything on the 27th November every year, The Church of Stop Shopping works less to advocate attempts to withdraw from corporate consumption as a continuous year-round general strategy and more as a promotional tactic to create discursive space for rethinking the relations of consumption.[6] The publicity that Reverend Billy and the Church have gained in the USA and the UK in particular means that it works as a 'lever' or promotional tool to generate consideration of the effects of what consumers buy on them/ourselves, on the people who produce the goods and the environment; on the ties and alliances in question. Beyond this, its recommendations are either undefined or 'open', depending on your point of view, although a variety of potential actions are pointed towards: lessened consumption, alternative forms of consumption (second-hand swap shops), and unionized activity.

In turn, this begs further questions about not only what other types of change are imagined across the spectrum of contemporary anti-consumerist discourse as happening 'after the boycott' or 'after the action' but also *how* these changes are imagined as emerging. Some of the contradictions about how change is imagined as potentially coming-into-being are, perhaps, laid out most starkly in the activities of the Canadian-based anti-consumerist organization, activist network and magazine publisher Adbusters.

Meme machines and viral vanguards

Adbusters describes its activities as 'tinkering with the corporate genetic code'. One of the best known anti-corporate organizations, it is most famous for its subvertising and culture jams: spoof adverts of corporate behemoths such as Nike, Marlboro and Calvin Klein, many of which appear in its eponymous not-for-profit magazine. Founder Kalle Lasn frequently invokes the cybernetic metaphor of 'memes' – the Richard Dawkins-derived concept, prevalent in digital theory, which describes ideas jumping, contagiously, in bio-hyperlink fashion, from one head to another (Dawkins 1989; Terranova 1996; Blackmore 2000). What we need, Lasn states, is

> the ready for prime-time metameme – the big paradigm-busting idea that suddenly captures the public imagination and becomes a superspectacle in itself ... the meme-warfare equivalent of a nuclear bomb. It causes cognitive dissonance of the highest order. It jolts people out of their habitual patterns and nudges society in brave new directions.
>
> (Lasn 1999: 124–5)

In the cyberrevolutionary machine, Adbusters can be positioned as a kind of viral vanguard, the evolutionary fittest pushing forward the almost-inevitable revolution. The nature of media influence is frequently described in overtly hypodermic terms ('The commercial mass media are rearranging our neurons, manipulating our emotions ... So virtual is the hypodermic needle that we don't feel it' Lasn 1999: 12). Just as Lasn's cyberhumans have been programmed, they can be deprogrammed by the apparently irresistible revolutionary force of the ultimate culture jam. This is the viral vanguard of an inevitable anti-consumer revolution, one speaking the language of cyber-revolution merged with Situationist anti-consumerism.

This rhetoric carries traces of the model of the brainwashed, zombie-consumer. It is a model which can be tracked from modernism's characterization of the duped and deluded masses (as Andreas Huyssen discussed so eloquently) through to Vance Packard's classic 1950s text on advertising's *Hidden Persuaders* and Guy Debord's *The Society of the Spectacle*; and at its worst, such perceived automaton behavioural patterns can work to stoke the self-righteous elitism of the all-seeing few (Packard 1957; Debord 1967/1994; Huyssen 1987). It is a language which also appears, in ironic form, in Reverend Billy's sermon: 'I believe that this will deprogram a consumer in the middle of a pseudo hip sip' (Talen 2003: 6). As Don Slater discusses in *Consumer Culture and Modernity*, there is a strain in theories of consumer culture as spectacle which both 'tend to produce highly totalized images of consumer society', and which 'appeal to a kind of libidinal self and body still lurking under the many layers of commodification and passivity' (Slater 1997: 126–7). The notion is of an unproblematically innocent consumer who is either placed 'inside' or 'outside' a hermetic system which appears to be produced in a zone beyond human agency. Such a paradigm can often inform Adbusters' rhetoric.

Yet at the same time, Lasn's is a social constructionist view of the world, an understanding which swerves between simplistic binaries of heroic viral vanguards and brainwashed cultural dupes, and sophisticated gestures towards a multifaceted, hegemonic, war of attrition, in which campaigning for change is all about 'finding the leverage point' (Lasn 1999: 131). This approach connects to other campaigns such as to the populist, coalition-building strategy of French farmer José Bové and the Confederation Paysanne in their actions against the McDonaldization of French food and discriminatory American trade tariffs; which, by engaging with movements, popular issues and existing political systems, built successful alliances between anti-corporate activists, conservative citizens in Middle France, New Delhi farmers and local co-operatives (Bové and Dufour 2001; Littler 2002). Lasn's discourse therefore oscillates between assertions of the 'hypodermic' nature of media influence (and proposing a communal utopia which can sound almost feudal) to complex analyses of the workings of late capital, strategic policy suggestions and ideas for creating alliances.

This, then, is an anti-consumerism which swerves between reductive vanguardism and an innovative and sophisticated politics of complexity (calling, for example, for 'infodiversity' as well as 'biodiversity'). In addition,

Adbusters has also been an energetic proponent of a range of actions designed to provide actually existing alternatives to corporate consumer culture, from its anti-Nike ethical footwear initiative (the 'Black Spot Sneaker') to alternative forms of media (Littler 2004; Adbusters 2006). The future paradigms it gestures towards often focus on economic and environmental sustainability, which, they argue, should be achieved by the shift in public consciousness, by rewriting legal definitions of corporate behaviour and by unashamedly large-scale planning. Lasn, citing the Index of Sustainable Economic Welfare (ISEW) developed by Herman Daly and John Cobb, argues that we 'need more than "small do-goody gestures" for the environment – start teaching a whole new economic paradigm, design cities with pedestrians and public transport in mind' (Lasn 1999: 89–90, 112). This is combined with suggestions for political-legal strategies for change:

> We must rewrite the rules of incorporation in such a way that any company caught repeatedly and wilfully dumping toxic wastes; damaging watersheds; violating antipollution laws; harming employees automatically has its charter revoked, its assets sold off and the money funnelled into a superfund for its victims.
>
> (Lasn 1999: 157)

Adbusters can therefore be reflexive enough to put suggestions for changes to the law, and to regulation, on the agenda. Similarly, an often overlooked feature of *No Logo* is the extent to which Klein explicitly refers to the need to engage with other 'political solutions' beyond boycotts (Klein 2000: 442). As consumer boycotts are not enough, and company codes of conduct are not to be trusted, what we need, she argues towards the end of the book, is an updated version of union activity on a global scale:

> In the twenties and thirties, when the crises of sweatshops, child labor and workers' health were at the forefront of the political agenda in the West, these problems were tackled with mass union-isation, direct bargaining between workers and employers and governments enacting tough new laws. That type of response could be marshalled again, only this time on a global scale, through the enforcement of existing International Labour Organisation treaties, if compliance with those treaties were observed with the same commitment that the World Trade Organisation now shows in it enforcement of the rules of global trade.
>
> (Klein 2000: 438)

What is hoped for are governmental and international laws enforcing union-style curbs on the excesses of global capital (although it also leaves the door open for the possibility of creating new modes of non-capitalist business). These possibilities, Klein's narrative implies, will hopefully be achieved through interconnections between activists in the embryonic movement-of-movements, which is where *No Logo* most explicitly locates the agency for change. Hopes of reclaiming citizenship over consumption, creating public space and common ownership and greater global parity of resources are invested in the forging of links between very different groups: the workers in export processing zones, culture jammers, ageing academics and anti-corporate campaigners; and so the book ends by repeating the Reclaim the Streets slogan 'the resistance will be as global as capital' (Klein 2000: 443–6). Klein's call is effectively making links beyond that of consumption: it points to how we need reflexivity as citizens as well as consumers.

Imagining anti-consumerism

I have been discussing how, in these particular cases, the role of anti-consumerist activism, the status of its consuming audience and cultural change are imagined. In terms of activism, *No Logo* enacts a politics in which change is ultimately conceived of as happening through global laws, brought about through the movement-of-movements. It displays a somewhat contradictory attitude towards its own role as activist-text. Adbusters argues, energetically, for large-scale social change by forming new principles of economic and environmental sustainability, and it imagines such change has the best chance of being brought about through ideological and discursive shifts. Roddick's imagined change will happen variously through activism, legal changes and individualized consumer power. Here Roddick represents an interesting faultline in anti-consumerism; for, on the one hand, she and the Body Shop have hugely popularized the issue of trade ethics, having a large discursive impact and extending the appeal of ethical consumption; and, on the other, it is clearly not a co-operative organization, but a capitalist enterprise that does not use the International Fairtrade Mark and seeks to set its own rules for its own brand of 'ethical trading' (a fact made only too apparent through its 2006 takeover by the giant cosmetics corporation L'Oréal). Reverend Billy's church makes specific, vivid performances against consumerism and gestures towards some alternatives, but for the most part it leaves future systems of consumption open or undefined.

Both the type of consumer and anti-consumer being imagined, and activism's relationship to them, differ in these modes of anti-consumerist activism. *No Logo* interpellates its audience of youthful Generation X consumers by gesturing emotively towards a shared habitus. Anita Roddick's work has primarily talked to a rational-choice consumer who needs to be educated into further change, towards which *Take it Personally* points as a didactic primer. Adbusters' discourse can both imagine itself as viral vanguard waking up the duped masses, and can operate in more sophisticated strategic ways, not as the inevitable future victor, but rather as a tactical spanner in the cultural works that brings together coalitions and alliances to strike at points of neoliberal vulnerability and to attempt to fashion alternatives. Reverend Billy's church simultaneously addresses anti-consumers and consumers saturated with postmodern irony and activist ennui and anti-consumers and consumers who at some level need to have their attachments to dreams of consumer wholeness broken.

Relational reflexivity

We have looked at what these anti-consumerist discourses understand as 'activism', at how they understand their own role in relation to it, at the narratives they produce about how change happens, and at how the implied consequences or futures beyond anti-consumerism are imagined (or not). In other words, we have looked at how 'reflexive' such discourses are about their own positions and context. To extend this discussion, here I want to highlight some of the varied yet interconnected understandings of that fraught and richly suggestive term, 'reflexivity'. In particular, I want to draw on the work of Scott Lash, Donna Haraway and Bruno Latour, as their nuanced writings appear to me to open up interesting further ways to think about the implications of how reflexivity 'works' in these texts and movements, and of the problems and possibilities of the anti-consumerist discourses I am discussing.

Scott Lash's (2002) book *Critique of Information* develops his earlier arguments about reflexivity (Beck *et al.* 1994; Lash and Urry 1994) as a vital, constitutive feature of the technological present. In the post-Fordist information society, reflexivity is no longer something which takes place in a separate, rareified (or reified) dimension of time and space from the everyday:

> Reflexivity in the technological culture is not a separate process of reflection. There is no time, no space for such reflection. There is fusion of words and things, of thought and practice. To think is not just at the same time to do; to think is at the same time to communicate. In the technological culture, reflexivity becomes practice; it becomes communication.
>
> (Lash 2002: 18)

Reflexivity in contemporary technological culture and life, then, is instantaneous, is immanent to being (and Lash is very alive to how this techno-social landscape is fissured depending on a given person's location and access to social and cultural capital). The time and space for separate reflection, a constitutive experience for privileged 'moderns', have collapsed. In articulating this paradigm, Lash both draws on a variety of theorists – particularly Deleuze and Derrida – who have problematized and sought to erase the distinction between representation and object, and positions the generation of such theories as themselves being indicative of this social and cultural age. The generation of affective becomings becomes a key characteristic of this technoscape of informational reflexivity.

This provides a useful way to further our understanding of *No Logo*'s reflexivity. For example, returning to the passage I quoted earlier, when Klein recounts that '[m]any of the battles we fought were over issues of "representation" – a loosely defined set of grievances mostly lodged against the media, the curriculum and the English language', we might read this as much as anything, as the bemoaning of the outdated methodology of a previous era: as a *critique of representation* itself. Certainly the activist-text structure of the book, and its enormously successful performance *as information*, embody precisely the type of reflexive information Lash is discussing: it responds rapidly; it responds with inbuilt reflection; and it conspicuously generates information and affect. In these terms, *No Logo* becomes a paradigmatic anti-consumerist text of the information society.[7]

However, if 'reflexivity' has been understood, as here, as a driving and constitutive feature of modern informational society, it has also been understood, in a second, very different way, as a means of generating, or coming to elaborate upon or 'know' the self, as discussed for example in the work of Ulrich Beck and Anthony Giddens (Beck *et al.* 1994). Giddens' analysis of the generation of individualized forms of reflexivity has been taken up as a useful tool by academics in cultural studies, for example, to understand contemporary lifestyle magazines (Gauntlett 2002). Giddens' paradigm of reflexivity tends to foreground atomized and intensely individualized forms of sociality, from which 'reflexivity' can offer itself up to be understood as a relatively bounded form of narcissistic individualism (Giddens 1991), and the stories of Anita Roddick reflecting on her own self, her own heroic position, are perhaps particularly suited to being understood in these terms.

Yet this second sense of being 'reflexive' does not necessarily primarily involve reinforcing hyper-individualized social relations. We might, for example, think of the strong tradition, particularly shaped in cultural studies through feminist and postcolonial theory, of 'reflexivity' involving a discussion of the situated position of the academic-author-self in relation to the subject under scrutiny. Broadly, such reflexivity involves scrutinizing the situatedness of the author as an attempt to evade the fallacy of Enlightenment-derived scientific objectivity: both to reject its positivist empiricism and to break from the brutal historical baggage of its derogatory classifications of otherness (Clifford 1988; hooks 1990; Haraway 1997: 198–304; Harding 2003). To *not* engage in such reflexive actions means, in effect, to collude to some extent with this tradition and its fantasies of transcendental authority. For many cultural studies scholars, making gestures towards or working from the position of a reflexive practice is a basic tenet of the discipline, as for a connected branch of social science, as outlined by Bourdieu and Wacquant in *An Invitation to Reflexive Sociology* (1992). This kind of reflexive writing also carries the risk of self-indulgent narcissism and of valorizing expressions of 'experience' which emerge from 'the self' as of somehow greater validity than other discourses. It carries the risk of potentially ignoring both questions of psychology and the unconscious, and re-importing 'objectivity' through a conduit of possessive individualism.[8] But its implications, as Lash puts it in *Reflexive Modernisation*, are also that 'reflexive human science would need to understand itself as just another ethnomethodology'. Whereas '[f]or Beck and Giddens it tends to involve the bracketing of the life-world to arrive at individualised, subject-object forms of social knowledge', this perspective 'involves bracketing subject-object knowledge and situating knowers in their life-world' (Beck *et al.* 1994: 156).

In her book *Modest_Witness*, after noting how the separation of expert knowledge from opinion was a founding gesture of modernity (Haraway 1997: 24), Donna Haraway moves on to think through some of the problems with being reflexive, in this way, observing Bruno Latour's reluctance to engage with a reflexive methodology because it seems to him to simply be a way of reproducing more of the same subject position. From here, Haraway makes the suggestive point that, as reflexivity could be thought of as simply ending up at the same position, instead '[d]iffraction, the production of difference patterns, might be a more useful metaphor for the needed work than reflexivity' (Haraway 1997: 34). This, she argues, can help any kind of programme which

> is committed as much to knowing about the people and positions from which knowledge can come and to which it is targeted as to dissecting the status of knowledge made.
>
> Critical reflexivity, or strong objectivity, does not dodge the world-making practices of forging knowledges with difference chances of life and death built into them. All that critical reflexivity, diffraction, situated knowledges, modest interventions or strong objectivity 'dodge' is the double-faced, self-identical god of transcendent cultures of no culture, on the one hand, and of subjects and objects exempt from the permanent finitude of engaged interpretation, on the other.
>
> (Haraway 1997: 36–7)

Haraway's model, in effect, highlights and extends the possibilities of thinking reflexive positionality and knowledge-production as relational and temporal processes, and as imbricated in complex, contingent conjunctures, distributions, systems and networks of power. This connects back to Bourdieu's ideas about reflexive methodology as an anti-individualist strategy, a means of thinking how 'persons at their most personal are essentially the personification of exigencies actually or potentially inscribed in the structure of the field, or, more precisely, in the position occupied within the field' (Bourdieu and Wacquant 1992: 44). It emphasizes the *relationality* of reflexivity beyond the confines of a reflexivity which is solely anchored in individualism, by focusing on the nature of the alliances through which the individual is constituted and situated. Emphasizing *relationality* also has a resonance with what Judith Butler also gestures towards in her text *Precarious Life*, when she argues, (focusing on feminism) that

> It seems more crucial than ever to disengage feminism from its First World presumption and to use the resources of feminist theory, and activism, to rethink the meaning of the tie, the bond, the alliance, the relation, as they are imagined and lived in the horizon of a counterimperialist egalitarianism.
>
> (Butler 2004: 41–2)

Both Butler's and Haraway's understandings open up more ways of engaging in what we might highlight as 'relational reflexivity', and this, as I have been attempting to demonstrate, can help refine an understanding of the work of these contemporary anti-consumerist texts. It can help us think about whether, and how, the situated and specific nature of these knowledges and understandings being brought to anti-consumerist interpretations are being recognized; of how these understandings change in the process of 'activism' and travel somewhere else, become 'defracted', become different.

This can also help us see how it is not particularly helpful to simplify 'anti-consumerism' as a monolith. For if an awareness of the role of popular discourse in shaping the citizen-consumer can be found, so too can romanticizations of activist enclaves which shore up its boundaries; if there are spaces where consumers are shaped as dupes, there are also sophisticated understandings of the affective investments and complex psychologies of consumer identities. Identity politics or reflexivity in anti-consumerist texts can work to focus on the nature of the ties between consumers and producers, between consumer behaviours and to sketch mattering maps which engender alliances. This is partly how they gain their power; it can be the source of great affective reflexive strength, or the source of a more narcissistic reflexivity. They appear to be most persuasive, we might say, when they emphasize the nature of a particular alliance in question and reflect on their own positioning or standpoint; when the connections between consumers are considered as well as the connections between consumers and producers; and when the interconnections between interior and exterior economies, and between affective and material currencies, are foregrounded. Anti-consumerist discourse is at its most effective when it is relationally reflective enough to be articulated to popular interests to form counter-hegemonies, and when it can create affective mattering maps with those who can link to their various modes of *habitus*. In other words, the more relationally reflective anti-consumerist texts are, the better, as it renders them the more open to making more, and more egalitarian, alliances.

Postscript: beyond the boycott

In his book *The Politics of Nature*, Bruno Latour moves beyond thinking about how a phenomenon (here, 'nature') has wildly variable historically and cultural specific formations to unearthing, radically problematizing and dispensing with the very category itself (in effect, doing for 'nature' what Judith Butler did for 'gender'). Instead, he suggests a complex schema for bringing its disaggregated elements – as part of 'the sciences' – into democracy. And in this radically reconstituted version of 'democracy', what will play 'an indispensable political part' is economics:

> The simplistic character of which economics is so often accused becomes on the contrary its most striking quality, the only one that can produce a scale model of the common world. Thinking they had come across an instance of self-regulation, the adherents of natural equilibria made a small mistake on the placement of the prefix 'self'. Yes, economics is a self-reflexive discipline, but it does not designate any *self*-regulated phenomenon: it simply allows the public to see itself, to conceive itself, *to constitute itself as a public*.
>
> (Latour 2004: 150–1; italics in original)

In this paradigm, economics will have a role in which it will no longer appear specialized in an abstract sense but will rather be a means by which we will make sense of our collective lives.

Whether we agree with the viability of Latour's elaborate schema or not, it is a very suggestive image; one which, in its own, inimitable, fashion, has something in common with the growth in studies of cultural economy (du Gay and Pryke 2002; Amin and Thrift 2004; Merck 2004). These studies – thinking through, for example, the always-already 'culturalized' dimensions of 'the economy', and emergent working practices in the post-Fordist creative industries – have developed new ways of interrogating the old question of how economic/cultural form shapes social identities, possibilities and life opportunities in a climate in which cultural economies have adopted distinctive new forms. What I have been implicitly suggesting in this chapter is that there is, equally, much to be gained from thinking through the problems and possibilities of anti-consumerist activist discourse by using some of the theoretical tools offered by cultural studies and these adjacently networked disciplines of cultural economy and cultural theory. Theorizing anti-consumerist activism is just as important as theorizing new formations of trading floors, consumer debt or the fluctuating fortunes of advertising agencies. This is particularly the case as studies relating to anti-consumerist activism, particularly on co-operative movements and boycott cultures can tend to focus very heavily on historically oriented economic questions, and the little study of contemporary anti-consumerism there is available can understandably at times tend to be overly celebratory. Using and extending cultural studies' models of articulation and transformative practice can open up more possibilities for useful critical interrogation.

This chapter has attempted to use such an approach while bringing theories of (and relating to) cultural economy and consumer culture into dialogue with contemporary anti-consumerist discourses. While, in the past, it has been extremely useful to consider models of representation (such as the colonialist imagery of the Body Shop), it is perhaps now just as important for cultural studies to start engaging in the wider, much more messy and complex terrain which anti-consumerism occupies beyond representation; a terrain which includes how alternative economies elicit affectual investments (or not), and the social, theoretical and political economies – which are always, in their various forms, always-already cultural – of what is imagined as possibly happening after the action or boycott. Thinking about to what extent anti-consumerist discourses are relationally reflexive, I have been suggesting, is one of the many possible ways of doing this; that in attempting to extend *beyond* boycott cultures, it is often most productive to, at one and the same time, pay attention to investments and lives lived *during* (and *before*) them. As cultural studies and the movement-of-movements remind us, acknowledging investments, contingencies and fallabilities can often work as a crucial means of engendering openness and creating further alliances; and if, in Latour's terms, 'the global economy' is one means by which the collective can 'see itself', then much might be gained from reflexively interrogating anti-consumerist cultural economies too.

5 Ecologies of green consumption

> Climate change has become a dinner-table conversation everywhere.
> (Marianne Barner, Head of IKEA in Sweden, Barner 2007: 59)

Over the past few years, contemporary 'turbo' levels of consumption have increasingly become presented as seriously environmentally problematic, affecting areas both close to and far from home. Newspapers present us with images of 'dead seas' filled with garbage; television programmes air anxieties about plastic bags and patio heaters; journalists report that new power plants are being opened every week to cater for global production. Some of the most high profile responses to this have been attempts to 'green' consumption. Recycling is a hot topic, an increasing number of products are marked as 'green', we are offered 'carbon neutral' services, are told to consume less and sold organic goods and 'bags for life'. And yet attitudes towards such attempts to 'green' consumption are often sceptical and the subject is often shot through with contradictions. Green consumption is everywhere: and yet it is a slippery, multifaceted and often apparently contradictory subject.

This chapter approaches the question of what green consumption is and to what extent it might be thought to offer useful or 'radical' solutions to contemporary interconnected environmental problems. The first section outlines some contemporary contexts for green consumption, including global warming, peak oil, biotechnology and pollution, discussing these issues both in relation to popular anxieties and the emergence of niche markets. The second section suggests that one particularly useful set of terms to use to theorize contemporary green consumption and its contexts is Félix Guattari's work in *The Three Ecologies,* and so sketches his theory of 'eco-sophy'. Broadly speaking, Guattari demands that we think the psychological, the social and the environmental together, that we consider the connections and disruptions between them, and suggests that practices and discourses which do not connect them cause profound inequality and danger.

By bringing these two sections together, the third part of the chapter attempts to apply Guattari's theories to create one understanding of green consumption within what cultural studies likes to term 'the contemporary cultural conjuncture' (see, for example, Hall *et al.* 1978; Grossberg 2005). (In fact, as we will see, such an approach is in some ways fairly congruent with *The Three Ecologies,* as both attempt a contextualized, multifaceted and interwoven view of their subject.) It does so by suggesting that we might schematize contemporary 'ways of being a green consumer' into three key areas (buying 'green' products, recycling and consuming less) and then by discussing some of the most problematic disjunctions between social, mental and environmental ecologies at work in these realms of consumption. In effect, then, the chapter uses *The Three Ecologies* as a tool to help dissect the various reasons for paradoxes and contradictions within the realm of green consumption. In the process, it argues for an interconnected or 'ecosophical' approach to its analysis, regulation and practice.

Some contemporary contexts of green consumption

How might we begin to understand the contemporary surge of interest in being – however partially, paradoxically or hypocritically – a green consumer? Such a growth in interest in green consumption can be explained through a number of different contexts, which are often closely imbricated together: the issue of climate change and the activities of the environmental movement; the expansion of corporate niche markets; the question of increasingly 'toxic' or degraded environments; and peak oil. Let us look briefly at these issues in turn.

Climate change

The heightened nature of awareness and anxiety about climate change and global warming is one obviously crucial driver of green consumption. We are encouraged, for example (although many would say we are not encouraged enough, or are not provided with the facilities *to be able* to do this enough) to switch to long-lasting light bulbs, to dump the car and use public transportation, to consume products that can be recycled, to recycle many of the products we buy, to consume energy from renewable sources and to fly less. Anxieties that the planet will be, at best, profoundly unpleasant through the perpetuation of current rates of warming (through extreme temperatures, scorched earth, wide-ranging floods, species extinction and large numbers of human deaths), and, at the worst, that this process will cause feedback loops leading to an uninhabitable planet are taken increasingly seriously, even if relatively little in proportional terms has actually been done about it. In the world's richer, powerful states, awareness of climate change has been registered through both media coverage and changes in experience, which, while very different from the much more forceful effects hitting poorer nations first (Simms 2005) are nonetheless already tangible, in particular through erratic and 'unseasonal' weather (such as the 2003 heatwave in France and the 2005 hurricane in New Orleans).

Simultaneously shaping – and shaped by – this experience of 'strange weather' is an expanding media discourse about environmentalism.[1] This spans an extremely wide spectrum: from the reportage of melting glaciers in glossy magazines like *Vanity Fair*, through newspaper coverage of the UK-government commissioned 2006 Stern Report into Climate Change, to blockbuster films like *The Day after Tomorrow* and *An Inconvenient Truth* (Emmerich 2004; Guggenheim 2006; Stern 2006; *Vanity Fair* 2007). A recent study by Boykoff and Goodman notes an upswing in media coverage around the time of the Kyoto Protocol in 1997 and an overwhelmingly dramatic increase in the media coverage of green issues from the mid-2000s (2008: 8–9). The 'peak' of media coverage of climate change *denial* (a PR practice itself funded, as many are now aware, by the petrochemical industry, largely Exxonmobil and its sponsored subsidiaries) appears to have passed (Monbiot 2007a: 23–7).[2] There are, in short, an increasing number of discourses and experiential indicators around that make it harder to avoid thinking and feeling about these issues, whatever may be thought and felt about them.

Cultural sociologist Noel Castree has assessed how this contemporary 'moment' of environmentalism is viewed as 'a cause' by comparing it to other moments in the history of environmentalism and analysing its reception by mainstream politics, business and the public. While the environmental movement had a 'thrilling late 1960s infancy and a rather successful 1970s adolescence', he writes, its development was thoroughly arrested in the 1980s and 1990s when it was stalled by the 'likes of Reagan and Thatcher'. By contrast, environmentalism is now big news again in the world's most powerful states, and politicians on the left and right want to be seen to engage with its agenda (Castree 2006: 11–21; see also Castree 2005). This clearly remains the case with many recent political gestures: in 2007, for instance, US President George Bush suddenly announced he had 'always' been involved with green issues, and one of the first subjects the newly-elected right-wing French President Nicolas Sarkozy talked about was 'the environmental agenda', by suggesting that a UN-steered world environmental organization be created (Tisdall 2007; White House 2007).[3]

Castree's question is: is this contemporary moment an unprecedented opportunity for environmentalism or a false dawn? For Western environmentalism is, as he puts it, 'a movement of paradoxes: it appears to exert real societal influence, whilst in practice being mostly ineffectual' (Castree 2006: 12). These paradoxes take three main forms. The first paradox is that environmentalism has been on the agenda of ruling parties for many years, but not in a way most environmentalists would recognize; the second, as sociologist Klaus Eder puts it, is that 'the environmental movement no longer dominates discourse on the environment'; and a third is that the public increasingly cares but does not act. For Castree, this is primarily because, from the 1980s, 'ruling parties saw it as in their interests to appropriate the language of environmentalism, but to adopt the practical policies of its least threatening versions' (Castree 2006: 14). The language of environmentalism has therefore overwhelmingly been channelled to serve 'the cause of a specifically liberal, market-led form of environmental management in key Western states'.[4]

Neoliberal profit and post-Fordist niche markets

Castree's distinction, like that of Elder before him, is in this latter respect very similar to Timothy Luke's account of 'green governmentality' and to what Tim Forsyth and Zoe Young have in a recent edition of *Mute* described as a 'new green order' which they discern to be evolving 'before our fearful, blinkered eyes' (Luke 1999; Forsyth and Young 2007: 31). In this new green order, politicians such as Tony Blair, George Bush and Nicolas Sarkozy announce that debate over climate change should now begin and that the bigger policy debate about who should carry the burden of tackling the problem should start. But a highly delimited set of answers have already been sewn up:

> there seems to be a consensus among global elites about where to start (be afraid, be very afraid ... but always trust the government), how to address the challenge (change development patterns in the South to 'offset' carbon emissions produced by business as usual in the North), and who is responsible (mainly you and me). Real doubts and arguments are suppressed while market friendly 'solutions' are served up on a nice, glossy plate.
>
> (Forsyth and Young 2007: 29)

The 'new green order', in these terms, attempts to channel people's *fears* of climate change into endorsing one particular, neoliberal set of solutions: to continue market-led corporate expansion; to ramify divisions between economically powerful and weak countries; and to seek to gain approval and endorsement for these strategies by making climate change the problem of the 'individual' rather than by making governments or regulators effect significant policy changes through production and distribution.

To apply terminology from recent neo-Foucauldian work on governmentality (Bratich *et al.* 2003; Grossberg *et al.* 2003; Hay and Oullette 2008) to this account, the new green order is seen to involve burdening the individual with an overwhelming (rather than partial) responsibility for change, otherwise known as 'responsibilization'. This has significant implications for green consumption, as it implies that, by 'governing the soul' of the individual, by encouraging the idea that tackling climate change is down to the individual rather than corporations or governments, the green consumer might, in effect, be read as a means or conduit to perpetuate and endorse neoliberalism. We will examine this question of to what extent green consumerism is a conduit for neoliberalism, and the scope of action in relation to this scenario, in more detail later on.[5] For the moment, it is enough to note that 'the new green order', in which contemporary neoliberalism works to 'responsibilize' the individual, is one significant driver of contemporary green consumption.

A related aspect of this complex is the *form* such an expansion of corporate power has taken in terms of production and consumption. By this I am referring to a topic this book has already looked at in a variety of ways: the emergence of the fragmented niche markets – or 'mass specialization' – of post-Fordism. While 'green' or 'environmental' products have a long history, since the 1970s green consumerism has emerged as a significant, specialized and itself highly variegated niche market. The proliferation of 'alternative' and green products and sensibilities in the 1970s (such as Celestial Seasonings tea and *The Whole Earth Catalog*) became by the close of the decade seized upon and turned into commercial opportunities (if they weren't already, and expanded if they were), spawning megabrands like The Body Shop and influencing the packaging and advertising of numerous other commodities. Thomas Frank terms this process *The Conquest of Cool* (Frank 1997). For David Brooks, 'Bobos', or 'bourgeois bohemians' wed capitalist enterprise to a hippie bohemian countercultural aesthetic, becoming both paradigmatic of the *zeitgeist* and a powerfully influential 'new upper class' in the process (Brooks 2000). In such ways, 'alternative' and bohemian values came to fuel important elements of the culture of late or post-Fordist capitalism. Such fusions of bohemia, environmentalism and the niche markets of post-Fordist late capitalism provide a key backdrop to any contemporary story of green consumption.

Pollution and biotechnology

What other contexts have helped create a fertile climate for green consumption's growth? The rise of green consumption can also be related to anxieties about both environmental pollution and biotechnology. The expansion of organic and genetically modified-free products, for instance, is a by-product of rising levels of pesticides and the development of genetically modified crops and intensive farming, all of which have spawned sizeable health and taste concerns (Bové and Dufour 2001; Seyfang 2003). Genetically modified (GM) food is highly significant in terms of consumer campaigning: in the UK, for example, the anti-GM campaign is regarded as one of the consumer movement's most high-profile success stories in recent years. Despite a rapidly expanding commercial biotech industry, the high profile stories that circulated in the British media in the late 1990s, combined with

NGO/activist campaigning and a broad-based popular outcry resulted in a number of supermarkets dropping GM food, which is widely thought to have killed off most of the biotech food industry in the UK (HealthWatch 2000; Shaw 2002; Brown 2004; Lezaun 2004).[6]

Similarly, the meteoric global rise of organic food, particularly in Europe, reflects a widespread anxiety that industrialized countries have become over-industrialized (Bell and Valentine 1997: 51, 194–6; Soil Association 2007). 'Organic' indicates an idea of 'purity' and attention to provenance. Just as GM can be connected to a fear of technological change, so can organic products be articulated to nationalistic, ethnocentric or class-bound sense of 'purity'. And such forms of what we might call 'fetishised de-fetishisation' (Littler and Moor 2008) can act as a means of compensating the consumer for environmental, social and cultural losses. However, obviously organic, non-GM and environmentally friendly products and discourses do not *have* to be, and are not *always*, connected in such ways.

Peak oil and the energy crisis

Another key contextual factor as to why green consumption is expanding today is anxieties about the lack of resources traditionally used for energy consumption. Non-renewable energy sources that have largely been used to supply power to industrialized countries are in steep decline. Worldwide oil, gas and coal supplies are running out (in that order). There is fierce debate over whether oil production has already 'peaked', or whether this process is one which will take place over the next two decades, but little controversy that the actual process is happening (Monbiot 2007a: 55–7). The decline of gas is expected to follow a decade or so after oil, followed a decade or so later by coal. Discoveries of *new* sites for oil and gas already peaked in the 1960s (Simms 2005: 24–6).

Consequently, global prices for oil are rising and, as in the 1970s, there is a reconfiguration of global 'geometries of power' because of the 'huge and disruptive transfer of wealth which is taking place between oil-producing and oil-consuming nations' (Massey 2002; Davis 2006: 54). As Mike Davis points out, consumers paid $1.2 trillion more for oil in 2004 and 2005 than in 2003 (Davis 2006: 54). These price rises have triggered both protests (in Britain, for example, by the car lobby) and concerns (ranging from the US Department of Energy to environmental campaigners and corporations) that it will precipitate a worldwide economic depression and 'resource wars' over this increasingly scarce commodity (Simms 2005: 24–7; Campbell 2006; Monbiot 2007a: 56–7).

Meanwhile, 'cleaner' renewable energy systems move higher up the discursive agenda but remain chronically under-invested in; and some 'alternative' fuel solutions are themselves causing serious problems. Biofuels, for example – or the creation of transport fuels out of plant matter – are as problematic as fossil fuels in terms of the amount of CO_2 they emit, and the use of land to grow crops for fuel rather than for food is in itself more than problematic, as it has both pushed the price of many foodstuffs up beyond levels of affordability and has resulted in large amounts of forest clearance (Monbiot 2007a: 157–61). Palm oil, for instance, is the cheapest commodity to produce as a biofuel. Its production for use in cars has resulted in widespread forest clearances across Indonesia (where as a recent UN report pointed out, it threatens the orangutan with extinction) and Malaysia, where it has been responsible for 87 per cent of deforestation between 1985 and 2000 (see United Nations 2007; Friends of the Earth in Monbiot 2007a: 159). These factors have all stimulated forms of consumption that are less dependent on non-renewable energy. These include consuming food that uses few food miles, or does not rely on large energy-guzzling heated greenhouses to grow (i.e. seasonable and local food), switching to renewable forms of power (such and wind and solar), or cycling and using trains and buses rather than driving cars.

This sketch of key contexts provides a background to some of the reasons why there is a certain 'incitement to discourse' (to use Foucault's phrase) around green consumption at the present time. However, to theorize the subject in more depth, I want to turn to the combined theory of philosophy and ecology of Félix Guattari, or, as he termed it, 'ecosophy', as it enables some of these factors to be explored and interlinked in potentially productive ways. For what *The Three Ecologies* offers, I suggest, are interesting theoretical resources to understand contemporary neoliberalism's implicit tendency towards individual 'responsibilization' alongside the theoretical capacity to think of alternatives. Some strands of critical theory can have a tendency to simply carp without opening a space up for further movement. Guattari's work does not.

Theorizing green consumption

> It is not only species that are becoming extinct but also the words, phrases and gestures of human solidarity.
>
> (Guattari 2000/1989: 44)

While the analyst and critical theorist Guattari is best known for his collaborative work with Gilles Deleuze (particularly their two volumes of *Capitalism and Schizophrenia*, *Anti-Oedipus* and *A Thousand Plateaus*), later in his life he became extremely interested in ecology and stood as a Green parliamentary candidate in France (Deleuze and Guattari 1972/2004, 1980/2004; Genosko 2002: 18–23). *The Three Ecologies*, published in 1989 and fully translated into English in 2000, elaborates these theories. As he wrote the work at the cusp of the 1990s, it can be situated in relation to the contexts I have described above (for many of these themes were of course fully existent or emergent then). The work begins by reflecting on how our current period of intense techno-scientific transformations are generating an 'ecological disequilibrium' which, unless remedies are found, will 'ultimately threaten the continuation of life on this planet's surface' (Guattari 1989/2000: 27).

In *The Three Ecologies*, Guattari considers how, wherever we turn, we seem to confront the same 'nagging paradox':

> on the one hand the continuous development of new techno-scientific means to potentially resolve the dominant ecological issues and reinstate socially useful activities on the surface of the planet, and, on the other hand, the inability of organized social forces and constituted subjective formations to take hold of these resources in order to make them work.
>
> (Guattari 1989/2000: 31)

Humans have the resources to resolve the current ecological disequilibrium, and yet have not been able to get it together to deal with it. Guattari describes how any attempt to confront or cut through at this paradox will, by necessity, need to work through three different formations, realms or 'ecologies': environmental, social and mental. These ecologies cannot be disconnected, as they are so interrelated ('It is quite wrong to make a distinction between action on the psyche, the socius and the environment', 1989/2000: 41) and working towards beneficial environmental change means working through all these areas as we perform and construct our everyday (or not so everyday) existences. For instance, therefore, considering 'mental ecologies' involves not just individualized psychologies or subjectivities (Deleuze and Guattari having been famously critical of this kind of 'subjective conservatism' in *Anti-Oedipus*) but of broader social psychologies, or 'minds' (Guattari 1989/2000: 54; Deleuze and Guattari 1972/1992). Considering 'social ecologies' involves, for example, thinking of how it is increasingly illegitimate that 'profit-based markets' should regulate human social activities, 'for there is a range of other value systems that ought to be considered' (Guattari 1989/2000: 64). Considering 'environmental ecologies' means that environmentalism 'must stop being associated with the image of a small nature-loving minority' (1989/2000: 52); and so environmental ecology might as well be renamed 'machinic ecology'. Through such multiple approaches, 'the ecosophical problematic', Guattari writes, becomes 'that of the production of human existence itself in new historical contexts' (1989/2000: 34).

The Three Ecologies, in its insistence on thinking ecology expansively, as a part of broader lifeworlds and lifestyles, fits within a realm of thought that is sometimes termed 'deep ecology', although Guattari does not describe these connections to his work in the book (and within the Anglophone world the recent nature of these translations means that these linkages have not yet been made to any significant extent).[7] However, the work can be seen to depart from a major strand of this tradition, inhabited most fully and famously by Norwegian philosopher and green political activist Arne Naess, in three key ways. First, Guattari's view of the environment and the ecology is not one that reifies or essentializes 'nature' as separate from culture, humanity or technology, as deep ecology has sometimes been charged (Katz *et al.* 2000: xi). Second, deep ecologists such as Naess propound 'self-realization' as a core tenet, but *The Three Ecologies* offers a more critical and historical take on the very notion of the self by historicizing possessive individualism within the context of the rise of capitalist modernity (see Gare 2000: 212; cf. MacPherson 1962; Bauman 2000); instead, it suggests that we *reinvent* being together, as 'it is not only species that are becoming extinct but also the words, phrases and gestures of human solidarity' (Guattari 1989/ 2000: 44). This means that, for instance, mental and social ecologies for Guattari might mean inventing new formations of 'family' and living toge-ther (whereas for Naess it would be more likely to involve an individual from a more traditional nuclear family finding enlightenment alone out in a field). Third, his theory, while emphasizing interconnections (responses that address the problematic will be transversal, connecting all the ecologies) is defiantly anti-totalistic. Guattari is not interested in any idea of hermetic systems or hermetic solutions (or a 'stupefying and infantilising consensus' Guattari 1989/2000: 50; see also 2000: 34). This is in contradistinction to the Naess-inspired tradition, which is primarily interested in ecology as a *totality* (for one of many critiques of Naess on this front, see Katz *et al.* 2000: x–xi).

Critiques of *The Three Ecologies* are possible. Guattari's account of media, for example, will appear to anyone with any grounding in media and cultural studies to be reductive and one-dimensional. However, as I attempt to show in the next section, the framework is a suggestive one to 'think with' in the context of green consumption. In particular, the idea of paradoxes and contradictions within and across the various different ecologies can help facilitate a means of discussing how combined social, cultural and theoretical contexts might be considered together in order to make sense of green con-sumption and consumerism, its problems and possibilities.

Ecosophy and green consumption

Guattari's argument that without thinking the environmental, the mental and the social together we produce 'paradoxes' and more inequalities is particularly useful to relate to the contemporary expansion in green consumption as there are so many contradictions in this area. In what fol-lows, I use Guattari's concept as a kind of springboard to foreground para-doxes in green consumption. In particular, and by referring to the contemporary contexts I outlined earlier, I consider contradictions in three broad areas of green consumption: (1) buying 'green products'; (2) recycling; and (3) the act of 'consuming less'. These three areas of green consumption are clearly all interwoven and overlap with each other as well as between themselves (for instance, one reason objects are recycled is because we are consuming so many disposable and non-biodegradable objects). They are not the only issues we might place under this rubric, but they are key aspects of contemporary green consumption. By examining these areas in conjunction with Guattari's concept of paradoxes through and between ecologies, I want to try to identify and delineate some of their current contradictions.

Consuming green products

One immediately conspicuous problem with 'buying green' is the social and cultural divisions around it. 'Green' products have often come with a higher price tag attached and are therefore ripe to be critiqued as a lifestyle option for the privileged middle classes. (And *above* the middle classes, as the rise of branches of what we might call the 'eco-aristocracy' attest – witness aristocrat Zac Goldsmith editing the environmental magazine *The Ecologist* or Prince Charles' organic farms.) The recent expansion of green products has more thoroughly 'mainstreamed' them across a wider spectrum of the middle classes. In Britain, for example, organic food is available at the UK's most popular supermarket, Tesco; and in the USA, the Home Depot store has expanded its range of 'green' products (Williams 2007). But while envir-onmentally friendly and organic products are now more widely available and disseminated among social groups, green consumption is clearly still often oriented, and is more *available* to, those with greater social and material privileges. The much-trumpeted opening of the US-owned store Wholefoods in London's upper-class white enclave of Kensington in 2007 was one of the more graphic instances of these forms of social stratification.[8] The first paradox, or problem, with green consumption then is that it tends to remain a more highly priced option in the market, ramifying all the attendant social divides this can bring.

To put it in Guattari's terms, paradoxes or contradictions like this occur because there is a disjunction between the types of environmental and social ecologies at play. In other words, buying green products may encourage healthy environmental ecologies, but they might also – intentionally or unintentionally – promote destructive social inequalities. Importantly, these paradoxes do not *have to*, and do not *always*, exist. Therefore it is worth pointing out how some of these contradictions have, can or might be solved as well as produced. For instance, the higher price of many 'green' products is not the same across the board ('green' nappies, for example, in the form of re-usable re-usables, are often cheaper than disposables). Some critics would point out that the higher price of many green goods is higher in terms of the point of sale price, but not if we factor in the longer-term costs and expanded/ contracted choices, or what Levett calls 'choice sets' (Levett 2003; IPPR and Green Alliance 2006: 17).[9] For example, in these terms, organic 'saves' in the long run because it leads to less costly and damaging disease; bikes and lower-emitting cars save because they lead to less asthma, car accidents and pre-mature death through pollution. Such built-in costs are starting to be more widely considered; for instance, in Britain, in December 2007, the govern-ment instructed that the 'climate cost' of all policy decisions be factored into all reports, although whether these costs are taken notice of is a different issue (see Wintour 2007). In addition, markets that are subject to change set costs, and so such higher consumer prices are shaped through regulation. For example, as minimal product safety standards over 'toxicity' and pollution shift (such as with EU regulations over the legal amount of carbon dioxide emitted by fridges), the costs attached to the 'special' green product are minimalized as it in turn becomes normalized as a basic standard require-ment. Green consumption therefore does not *inevitably* reinforce stark social and cultural divisions, but at the moment it only too often tends to replicate or reproduce these hierarchies rather than being organized in such a way as to *undermine* them.

A second paradox of contemporary green consumption is highlighted by Noel Castree:

> Environmentalism is about much more than a thing called 'the environment' . . . there are still too many who regard 'green issues' as somehow separate from other domains of life. This way of thinking is what permits many people to salve their conscience by consuming products from The Nature Company whilst driving their children to school in a Range Rover.
>
> (Castree 2006: 12)

This paradox is the phenomenon of green consumption being separated off from other areas of people's lives and 'parachuted in' (whether to provide pleasurable green gratification and/or to salve consciences). This is perhaps one of the more glaring realms of contradiction (or hypocrisy, depending on your point of view). It is a contradiction that in part exists because green products are not only bought with the 'pure' or sole motive of saving-energy in mind: often they are bought because they are better tasting or more lux-urious. And this does not always necessarily mark what would be, in

Guattari's terms, the 'subjective conservatism' of highly individualized hedonistic consumption. Equally, such motivations can fuel the more socially beneficial forms of individual consumption that Kate Soper terms 'alternative hedonism', such as buying a bike both because you enjoy cycling and also want to contribute in a small way to lessening car pollution (Soper 2008). Indeed, in these terms, the very reasons for such 'contradictions' can also be a potential 'lever for change' (Barnett and Soper 2005).

As Castree argues, this 'separating-off' involves thinking of 'the environment' as a distinct and hermetic entity – rather than, as in deep ecology, being everywhere, permeating all life. This separation is produced because 'green' forms of consumption are often articulated to or imbricated with a system of consumer capitalism driven by the pursuit of profit and 'economic growth', and as such leads to a third, increasingly apparent paradox: the production and consumption of more and more stuff in the pursuit of 'being green'. One example here was the consumer scrum in 2007 for the £5 bag created by high-end fashion designer Anya Hindmarch, which featured the words 'I'm Not A Plastic Bag'. This sold out within hours in London, becoming a collector's item (up to £200 on eBay) and spawning imitators (including the pastiche 'I'm A Smug Twat') as well as numerous fakes or knock-offs sold by street traders on Oxford Street and local markets in Britain.[10] As Michael Maniates puts it, '"living lightly on the planet" and "reducing your environmental impact" becomes, paradoxically, a consumer-product growth industry' (2002: 47).

This third paradox, then, is that green consumption can operate as a motor of 'economic growth'. Clearly green consumption is not *a priori* an engine of late capitalism, as many co-operative experiments – from health-food shops like Park Slope in Brooklyn to energy providers like the Sydney Energy Cooperative – attest. But green consumption often is articulated to capitalism. One means of addressing this contradiction is to attack the notion of 'economic growth' itself, and to point out its destructive environmental impact of prioritizing the increase of companies' financial profit for shareholders over the common good, as it overwhelmingly involves increased production and energy consumption. This, for example, is both what Clive Hamilton did in his book *Growth Fetish*, a best-seller in Australia, and the line the former British head of Friends of the Earth Tony Juniper often took in media appearances when discussing how to tackle climate change (Hamilton 2003; Juniper 2004; see also Mellor 2006).

At another point in the spectrum, however, the possibilities of green consumption in *expanding* economic growth have also been emphasized. As Timothy Luke has persuasively demonstrated, this has been the Clintonite context from which Al Gore sprang and is the narrative he overwhelmingly deploys (Luke 1999: 121–51), even while his 2006 film *An Inconvenient Truth* has gestured, in somewhat woolly and ambiguous fashion, towards the need to have to selectively *reconceive* the notion of 'economic growth'. Partially supporting 'economic growth' can also be a discursive tactic strategically deployed by green activists to win consent: the argument that, for example, the renewable energy industry can provide more jobs can easily be connected to this idea (Bentley, in Murray, 1999: x–xv). Other voices in the green spectrum have argued that time needs to be spent pressing for immediate technocratic alternatives to curb global warming rather than attempting to dent one of the core ideological shibboleths of contemporary capitalism. As George Monbiot emphatically argues in *Heat*, if serious actions on renewable energy are performed immediately, it would be possible to halt global warming now through international, national, community and individual shifts in behaviour, through practices and policy shifts; in other words, while his suggestions involve in practice a shift away from prioritizing economic growth to such a full extent, his suggestions are primarily reformist in nature (though very significantly so). Either way, as Monbiot's remarkable book attests, and as even voices in alignment with 'the new green order' – such as Al Gore's – demonstrate, it is extremely hard to avoid some degree of engaging with the rethinking of 'economic growth' if attempting actually to tackle climate change (Monbiot 2007a, 2007b).

A fourth paradox is that a product can be 'green' in some aspects (such as through its discouragement of the continual use of plastic) but not in others, whether in the realm of environmental ecologies (the use of pesticides in non-organic fabric) or social ecologies (by using grossly overworked, underpaid and outsourced labour). The fact that Hindmarch's 'I'm Not A Plastic Bag' was produced in China using cheap labour and was produced neither using organic materials nor under fair trade conditions, for example, generated a considerably outraged if brief spurt of publicity in Britain. This is itself proof that these paradoxes are often very visible, and in turn can be mobilized to a number of different political ends, whether to extend 'green consumption' or reject it.[11]

In turn, this indicates a fifth paradox: the loose criteria for 'green' labelling and its potential use as a sales technique when the product might under scrutiny have precious little credibility on this front. For instance, a 2007 *New York Times* article discussed how US store Home Depot invited its suppliers to apply to have their products included in its 'Eco Options' campaign. Some 60,000 products were suddenly deemed to qualify (out of Home Depot's total range of 176,000), many on the most tenuous of criteria:

> plastic-handled paintbrushes were called nature-friendly because they were not made of wood. Wood-handled paintbrushes were promoted as better for the planet because they were not made of plastic. An electric chainsaw? Green, because it was not gas-powered.
> (Krauss 2007: 1)

This form of what Krauss calls 'overstated green marketing' can deploy a criteria so loose it becomes meaningless and of little help to sustainable environmental ecologies.

And a sixth and related paradox, already covered to some extent in Chapter 3, is when a company uses a small tokenistic investment in selling green products – such as organic, biodynamic or 'sustainable' consumption – to 'greenwash' its image. When the supermarket giant Wal-Mart, for instance, announced it was 'going green' in 2007, the strategy was widely perceived to be an attempt to deflect attention from the storm of bad publicity it faced, including Robert Greenwald's film *The High Cost of Low Price* and lawsuits filed against it for its employee-underpayment, sex discrimination and union-busting practices (Featherstone 2005; Spotts 2006; Haynes and Littler 2007). Clearly, while Wal-Mart's aim for 30 per cent energy reduction would be useful if it were fulfilled, the company is well known for making emotive and unspecific statements about generalized 'aims' and 'targets' without putting timeframes or goals to them. As Chris Kofonis from the Wake-Up Wal-Mart campaign put it:

> You have to look at what Wal-Mart does with an incredible degree of scepticism because this company has a history of saying one thing to main street and another thing to Wall Street. They say they're taking action to clean up the environment – that's a good thing. But which Wal-Mart is going to show up? The one that says it's improving healthcare benefits when they're actually getting worse? The one that says it pays good wages when in fact it doesn't?
>
> (Clark 2006)

Some alternatives to the paradox of greenwash have already been outlined in Chapter 3, most notably the lobbying for corporate social *accountability*. CSR debates on greenwash and these debates about overstated green marketing overlap in that, in both cases, the corporate commitment to 'being green' is minimal, tokenistic and loudly hyped while the company's larger-scale or structural practices remain unreformed. As a commentator in the *New York Times* article about Home Depot's reclassification scheme points out, if the company 'really wanted to promote sustainability, they would *discontinue* their products with the least green attributes' (Krauss 2007: 4). (This imagined action would be similar to British low-budget frozen food store Iceland's 1998 publicity campaign as 'the first UK store' to ban GM foods.) Or, as George Monbiot argues, supermarkets could stop using astronomical amounts of energy, rather than creating contexts where, in an ultra-brightly lit environment, banks of fridges and freezers with no doors do battle with heating, lighting and air conditioning systems. (Such a set-up uses so much energy so inefficiently that Monbiot says, 'it would be impossible to believe, if it were not by now one of the most ordinary facts of life', Monbiot 2007a: 192.)

There are, then, many different and often-conflicting meanings of 'green' in the context of green production. But equally these paradoxes are not inevitable ones. While no regulatory mechanism is ever going to be immune to criticism and contest, precedents exist for putting in place a minimum agreed definition of what certain types of green product means (such as the Soil Association's definition of 'organic' and 'non-GM' in the UK). It could be argued that this has the potential to be extended: that as a culture or cultures we can invent better definitions of 'green'. Let's now examine the contradictions of a different area: consuming less.

Complex simplicities: consuming less

Industrialized (and 'post-industrialized') countries are consuming more and more: per capita growth in consumption is for many resources expanding eight to twelve times faster than population growth (Princen *et al.* 2002: 4). This is not only because of increase in the number of marked new types of good, but also because the 'planned obsolescence' rate of products has speeded up and the culture of disposable goods has become more firmly entrenched. Juliet Schor's recent research, for instance, maps contemporary American 'turbo consumption' empirically through an examination of the changing dynamics of the clothing industry. While in 1991 the average American consumer purchased 34 pieces of apparel each year, by 2003 it was 57 (more than one new piece of apparel per week). This, Schor point out, is 'an increase of 23 pieces over a mere 12 years, or about two more each year, every year for more than a decade' (2006: 47). Such an expansion of consumer goods uses intensive energy and resources, not only through producing the goods themselves, but also through distribution and retail. One solution to the energy-producing, resource-sapping nature of the rapid turnover of commodities might therefore seem clear: just consume less.

In *The Sustainable Culture Reader*, Thomas Princen points out that while there is a lot of research on what consumers and citizens do, there is 'little research on not doing': on what they *don't* consume or buy (Princen, in Jackson 2007: 52). While this is true, it is less true than it used to be. There is a steadily increasing research literature on people and communities who consciously consume less than they could do (see, for example, Shaw and Newholm 2002) and Princen's own piece is part of an expanding area devoted to discussing the subject of 'consuming less' in more abstract, cultural, global and/or philosophical terms (see also Princen *et al.* 2002; Schor 2006; Thomas 2008). Indeed, in broader terms, it has recently become almost a truism for cultural and social critics to discuss the connection between high levels of consumption in the 'developed' world and relatively low – or lower than predicted – levels of 'happiness', personal satisfaction and fulfilment (see, for example, de Graaf *et al.* 2005; Layard 2006; Schor 2006; Barber 2007; James 2007).

The notion or practice of 'consuming less' is therefore an area of green consumption where a marked linkage between social, mental and environmental ecologies is already in circulation. For example, the idea that we are overwhelmingly collectively culturally conditioned to think that constantly purchasing new items is a primary source of pleasure (social/cultural ecology) and yet this practice, through high levels of production and consumption, harms the air that we breathe and the weather we experience (environmental ecology) and does not necessarily make us, after a while, any happier (mental ecology) is a central tenet of many recent journalistic and cultural commentaries. It is, for instance, the argument of the popular British cultural psychologist Oliver James' (2007) book *Affluenza*. Here the emphasis is on the cultural-psychological-mimetic) 'virus' that incites people, particularly in Anglo-American society, to consume increasing amounts while depression and mental illness rates skyrocket (James 2007). James' book is designed to act as a kind of social prescription for consumers to treat their 'disease'. Nor is James the first to use the term 'affluenza': in the USA, it is the title of a TV show and accompanying book devoting to helping people find practical ways to curb 'The American's habits of "buying, having and wasting too much"', or 'overconsumption' (de Graaf *et al.* 2005: xi, xix). More politically oriented analyses of 'affluenza' include *All Consuming*, written by Neal Lawson, the director of the British left think tank and pressure group Compass, and *Consumed*, penned by the popular American political scientist Benjamin Barber (Barber 2007; Lawson 2008).

Responses to 'affluenza' or consuming too much can be articulated in different directions: it has connections, as we shall see, with trends to 'downshifting' as a lifestyle option; links to the emergence of the 'slow' food movement (particularly in Italy); and roots in the 'voluntary simplicity' movement from the 1970s (particularly in the USA). Let us look at some of the problematic aspects, or contradictions, of these various different prescriptions for combating affluenza.

One problem of the practice of deliberately consuming less is that it is by definition an option practised by those with enough resources and cultural capital to be able to consume in the first place. The poor may be underconsumers, but this is rarely by active *choice*. This is why the 'voluntary simplicity' movement emerged from the world's most consumer-intensive country, the USA. Consciously reduced consumption is a practice pursued on the whole by those who could be more resource-intensive consumers if they chose to be: the practice arises primarily because they *choose* this path as a more 'enlightened', satisfying or less guilt-inducing alternative. To put it another way, if we were to draw on Abraham Maslow's 'hierarchy of needs', most consumer downsizers fit into the pattern of having their 'basic' psychological and 'safety' needs for food, water and shelter met and practise 'consuming less' as part of a move towards social respect and self-actualization (which is clearly different from, say the underconsuming ultra-poor in Puerto Rican shanty towns) (Maslow 1943).[12]

Indeed, many strands of 'consuming less' discourse, from Duane Elgin's self-help manuals which propounded voluntary simplicity in 1970s and early 1980s America, through programmes about contemporary yuppies seeking to 'escape' from the demands of high consuming lifestyles and downsize into a 'simpler' rustic way of life, to the slow food movement, state these aims of self-actualization and social respect explicitly (Elgin 1981; Parkins and Craig 2006; Thomas 2008). Such practices are limited to those who are affluent enough to *choose* these lifestyles. In these terms, consciously consuming less is practised by minority groups – producing a kind of 'enclave politics', rather than a politics more *widely distributed* through the population at large. Moreover, 'consuming less' discourses often overlook the question of class. As David Bosshart puts it, 'What the customer gets at Dollar Stores is the feeling of at least minimal empowerment, because Dollar Stores offer a mix of consumer products that even the poorest can afford' (2006: 12). Taken together, this shows how the social ecologies of consuming less, in other words, are on a global scale unequal and imbalanced.

A second paradox is that 'living more simply' can also connect to buying more. A good example here is the glossy US-based women's magazine *Real Simple*, which mixes articles on streamlining your life with ones on acquiring new possessions (such as a new fridge, noticeboard or walk-in wardrobe) in order to be able to carry out that process of 'simplification' more effectively.[13] In effect, we might say, it harnesses the discursive history of voluntary simplicity to try to get us to buy more Ralph Lauren. Again, as with buying green products, this strand of 'green consumption' here becomes, perversely, connected to the idea of buying more goods, using more energy and supporting the logic of economic growth.

A third problematic lies in the realm of the 'mental ecologies' of consuming less. Sometimes, for instance – as in the voluntary simplicity movement – consuming less can be presented as a very simple thing. This has a certain performative power, but from an analytic point of view obscures the complexity of relationships and dynamics around the subject. Moreover, it clearly is not always a very simple business to get everyone to consume less. Often it is very complicated. The ways people practise consuming less are not identical: they are extremely varied in social and cultural terms, from 'light-living' eco-aristocrats to 'back to the land' baby boomers, from metropolitan professionals trying to cut spending to European environmental activists. These, we might say, are complicated simplicities.

This complication is borne out in differing attitudes to consuming less. Consuming less is often presented, particularly in its more enclave forms, as a means of streamlining the soul, of finding greater happiness, pleasure and fulfilment. This narrative forms the basis of TV programmes that Lyn Thomas has described as 'eco-reality': which contain, in some form or other, the message that we should be living lives which are less consumer-focused and more oriented towards home-grown and often rural pleasures; and books about individual desires to downsize from the postmodern detritus of urban life, such as Meaghan Daum's novel *The Quality of Life Report*, in which a young woman moves from Manhattan to a quiet Midwestern town to find fulfilment (Daum 2003; Thomas 2008). In contrast, for commentators like Clive Hamilton, it is crucial to recognize that widespread consuming less will not be *pleasurable* so much as entailing 'a kind of death'. For Hamilton, it will mean that people have to *give up* some sources of pleasure (Hamilton 2007: 91–2); a position opposite to that of Kate Soper's formulation of different pleasures, or 'alternative hedonism' (Soper 2008). In these terms, we might say that the complexities of psychological and social attitudes to the subject are many and varied, and it is both unhelpful and disingenuous to treat it as anything less.

The more multi-faceted nature of the pleasures and problems of consuming less are now often grappled with in newspaper and magazine articles and columns in which journalists dispense lifestyle advice on consuming more sustainably or 'ethically'. In Britain, this has more or less become a journalistic micro-industry unto itself over the past few years. Leo Hickman's column in *The Guardian*, for example, which was later turned into a book, followed the progress of his family as they tried to live a greener, more sustainable lifestyle. As Clive Barnett *et al.* point out, such trends are part of a wider increase in news coverage of ethical consumption since the early 1990s which related to the emergence of a select number of organizations (like the Fairtrade Foundation and Soil Association) as credible sources of news (Barnett *et al.* 2007: 240). Such journalistic projects can provide a more social way of letting people know about options that are available; they can begin to discursively normalize the 'exceptional' or the 'enclave' practice; and they can offer versions of the changing psychological process or mental ecologies which people can *consider* – whether to adopt, adapt, reject or ignore – in relation to their own lives and practices. The disadvantages are that they can often assume a baseline social position (house ownership, for example, or sufficient income levels) and can be argued to offer wholly individuated solutions to problems of consuming less, thereby perhaps repeating some of the more individualizing tendencies of contemporary consumer society.

Recycling

So far we have reviewed key paradoxes and contradictions in two areas of green consumption: buying 'green products' and buying less. But what about recycling? The potential of recycling to save energy is now well known to be enormous. Recycling saves three to five times as much energy as incineration (the practice of burning waste). If Britain raised its rate to 70 per cent, it would make a carbon saving of 14.8 million tonnes; if there was simply a 1 per cent increase in recycling in the USA, it would reduce carbon dioxide emissions by an amount equivalent to taking 1.2 million cars off the road (Murray 1999: 101, 26, 6). That its potential is vast and untapped can easily be seen by any number of league tables that compare the recycling habits of different countries. In European league tables for instance, Britain can be seen to be dragging along the bottom with Greece and Portugal (only recycling 18 per cent of its municipal waste in 2006, primarily because of low levels of household recycling) while the Netherlands and Germany continually achieve the startlingly higher rates of 65 per cent and 58 per cent respectively (BBC 2005; Foley 2006; IPPR 2006).

All areas of green consumption are complex: recycling is perhaps particularly so. This is mainly because of the variety of materials and methods involved, and the slowness with which many (but by no means all) systems have been able to adapt and integrate using them. This means that, while some of recycling's paradoxes are 'environmental', to deploy Guattari's terms, the majority are 'social' and 'mental'. 'Environmental' paradoxes, for instance, include the issue that currently too much recycling actually involves 'downcycling', or creating only one or two further uses for the material before it arrives at landfill, as opposed to recycling it back into the same material and therefore using less energy (such as turning plastic cups into pencils rather than turning them back into plastic cups). This is a paradox that some environmental policy makers try to solve by 'closed loop' or 'cradle-to-cradle' thinking (see Braungart and McDonough in IPPR and Green Alliance 2006: 12). Put simply, such concepts emphasize a *continuity* of recycling, and its role in a wider context (of reducing, re-using and recycling) rather than conceiving recycling as a series of isolated actions or events. Such 'cradle-to-cradle' or 'closed loop' schemas therefore involve, for instance, a 'biological cycle', where all things that can be grown from the land are returned to the land (through compost) and a 'technical cycle' in which non-renewable resources are used and constantly recycled (rather than being allowed to 'escape' into landfill and incineration) (IPPR and Green Alliance 2006 : 12). This is what strategies of 'zero waste' – a target of a number of areas including San Francisco, Bath and New Zealand – have been attempting to move towards (IPPR and Green Alliance 2006: 6).

Another way of looking at these 'cycles' of objects is by borrowing Appadurai's concept, frequently used in cultural studies, anthropology and design history, of 'the social life of things' (Appadurai 1986). The idea that 'things have social lives', and that we might therefore chart the cultural journey of a dress from the store to the wearer to the second-hand shop, or the vase from kiln to gift to object of economic value, is suggestive for thinking about green consumption, or what we might call the 'green social life' of objects. It could, for example, be used to consider the economies of re-use at work in eBay, 'freecycle' networks or retro or charity clothing shops and to ask to what extent they either *incite* an increasing turnover of goods or conversely offer a means to *stem* the flow of energy required by the production of new goods (see Gregson and Crewe 2003; Hawkins 2006).

One key paradox of recycling is when objects are taken extremely long distances to begin their second (or third, or fourth) 'social life', thereby participating in a process of spewing out yet more carbon emissions in a supposed bid to save them, such as shipping plastics from the UK to China. Such events often spawn the most coverage by a gleeful right-wing press anxious to discredit anything 'green' because it might interfere with the 'free flow' of corporate business. Nevertheless, exporting recycling clearly remains a problematic paradox. Such contradictions are part of the wider picture of economic imperialism that affect production, with the zones of the world in which sweatshop and exploited labour are most predominant also tending to be those offering cheap, exploited labour in the recycling industries (often in highly toxic environments; see Ross 1997, 2006; Parks 2007: 38–9). Corporations wanting to use the 'secondary materials economy', such as recycled paper or aluminium, are not necessarily driven by long-term environmental consciences but by the search for shareholder profit. Countries and companies engaging in recycling but with low standards of labour regulation are therefore part of the same process of exploitation as with the production of cut-price running shoes, even if they are nominally part of the 'green economy'. This is the extreme example of an exploitative social ecology. Such practices are also created by a lack of fostering support for recycling facilities in the country sending its products abroad for recycling (Murray 1999).

This indicates that recycling's key problems and possibilities are bound up with issues of social organization. Nowhere is this clearer than when we look at nations' different recycling experiences and histories. For instance, Japan, Denmark and Holland all experienced the problem of not having enough land to continue using landfill, yet responded differently: historically, Denmark and Holland put their energies into recycling (this is why they are around the top of European league tables) while Japan put its energies into incineration (combined with a small number of token/model recycling villages; Murray 1999: 10–13). In the USA, recycling rates vary wildly: from some states averaging 8 per cent or under with other states over 40 per cent (and areas within them reaching 70 per cent) (Murray 1999: 105). In Britain, recycling is increasingly popular (commonly voted the most popular service in municipal polling) yet government has been slow to facilitate recycling opportunities (IPPR and Green Alliance 2006: 17), continuing to subsidize the incineration industry in an example of what to waste guru Robin Murray is indicative of the governmental failure to adjust to technological change and to shift from chronic short-term planning (Murray 1999: 70, 83, 87).

Such divergent experiences foreground the *range* of ways in which recycling systems can operate and the lack of *inevitability* about whether or not they are put into practice. Perhaps nowhere has this been clearer than in France, which in the 1990s as a nation moved abruptly from an incineration to a recycling strategy, largely through the influence of the French Green Party (Murray 1999: 113). Such an example illustrates the possibilities of shifting social systems of recycling and how this also requires combined psychological shifts. In Germany, for instance, where environmental issues have a long history of being placed high on the political agenda, recycling became extremely popular because it was perceived to have potential for expanding employment. 'Green collar jobs' in recycling, in the form of both the sorting and organizing of waste streams, and production in the 'secondary materials economy', have as a result become a significant source of employment in Germany (as opposed to less far-sighted practices of other European countries like Britain or Greece) (Murray 1999: 51). In the process, the German example shows how what Guattari would term 'mental ecologies' of recycling, or conceptual attitudes to recycling's role, is pivotal to whether and how it is adopted (or not) as a more widespread system.

Such 'mental ecologies of recycling' have also increasingly become a topic of interest for artists and academics as the subject of waste both moves higher up the political agenda and offers a suggestive means to explore a number of aesthetic, epistemological and ontological issues such as the boundaries of the human; the liminal, the overlooked and the out-of-sight; and the agency of 'non-human' actors (see, for example, Strasser 1999; Scanlan 2005). For example, Gay Hawkins' suggestive study *The Ethics of Waste*, which explores the various different micropolitical ethical and psychological investments in waste and recycling, highlights how objects being recycled 'are a product of social relations and affect them at the same time' (Hawkins 2006: 79). A number of fascinating art projects have also explored such issues, from the pioneering 1970s work of American artist Mierle Laderman Ukeles, who worked as the artist-in-residence for the New York Sanitation Department for 30 years (producing pieces such as *Maintenance Art*, which explored the overlooked nature of people and systems involved in waste disposal), to the *Stray Shopping Carts of Eastern North America* project, featured on the cover of this book, which dryly presents shopping trolleys as 'wildlife' to spot, and so as producing social-machinic ecologies of their own

(Finkelpearl 2001; Kastner 2002; Montague 2007).[14] What such work draws attention to are the crucial importance of psychological or 'mental' interactions with recycling, and the opening up of possible new ways of doing and being in relation to it.

At their least effective, then, strategies for recycling can facilitate more environmental damage (through, for example, the production of more carbon dioxide); an increase in social inequalities (through, for example, environmental imperialism); and ingrained conservative subjectivities (through, for example, singularly moralizing dogmatic approaches to the subject). At their most effective, they interlink social, environmental and mental ecologies to enable the lessening of environmental damage (through, for example, cutting carbon dioxide emissions), by reducing social inequalities (by, for instance, expanding jobs in recycling, or making rail transport more affordable than plane travel), and by letting a range of ways in which we might potentially connect to and practise green consumption open up.

Conclusion: an ecology of ecologies

This chapter has attempted to use Guattari's notion of 'the three ecologies' to explore some of the problems and possibilities of contemporary green consumption. I have not aimed to produce a comprehensive survey, but rather to identify key sites of contradiction in the main areas of green consumption – recycling, consuming less and green products – and to attempt to sketch the paradoxes in and between these zones. As we have seen, in the case of green production, some key contradictions at present lie in its separation of 'the environment' from wider social and cultural systems, especially through commodity fetishization; in how the selling of green products can be used, perversely, to drive economic growth, thereby inciting the use of more energy; and in the reproduction of other social divisions through, for example, high price and cultural capital. A key paradox of consuming less is that it is sometimes perceived as 'simple', when such simplicities are frequently complex, given their divergent relationships to pleasure and social position (ramified by how consuming less as a deliberate practice is pursued by the resource-rich). And in the case of recycling, key contemporary contradictions include poor social organization, whether on a local, national or international level; an over-expenditure of energy, whether through downcycling or exporting waste; and restrictive cultural/'mental' ecologies towards its practice, such as the failure to consider the extent of its potential for benefiting broader social and environmental ecologies, whether this be in terms of creating more jobs or improving air quality.

In the light of having discussed these paradoxes, it is useful to return to the issue of neoliberal governance and in particular the idea that in 'the new green order' individuals are responsibilized into dramatic yet ineffectual actions while corporations and the state shirk their responsibilities.[15] One counterweight to this perspective might be found in Robin Murray's point that in the UK 'householders are being asked to take more trouble in their handling of waste. They receive no financial compensation for doing so, yet they regularly press to extend it' (Murray 1999: 70). For Murray, this is an example of a kind of 'productive democracy' at work that local authorities and governments marginalize to everyone's loss. This perspective has a different emphasis from the analysis of the 'new green order' or green governmentality, which, we saw at the beginning of this chapter, emphasizes individuals as controlled and scapegoated rather than as potential levers for change.

Murray's approach introduces the possibility that individual/communal psychological desire to recycle is a *resource* which is too often ignored, rather than simply functioning as primarily an *imposition* on the populace who are being deluded into believing that their individual green activities are paramount (and in which neoliberal policy uses such public engagements with recycling as a diversion to carry on business as usual). As Gay Hawkins astutely points out in a discussion of Timothy Luke's work, such 'green governmentality' approaches can tend to posit a critical theorist who alone can see the truth while dismissing the activities of recyclers as little more than deluded false consciousness (Hawkins 2006: 111). By contrast, Hawkins herself emphasizes focusing on the micropolitics of affective engagements with waste, suggesting that productive forces can be found in noticing our small everyday interactions with it. She argues for a focus on the multiplicity of people's interactions with waste; on how bodily affects and habits of self-cultivation create an 'intersubjective ethos of politics' which occurs 'in conversations, in the media, in myriad relations in which practical examples of different ways of managing waste undermine normalised and exploitative practices and nurture receptivity to change' (Hawkins 2006: 127). These small actions and pleasures, she writes, are an important counter to prescriptive, top-down accounts of macropolitics, as they show how the minutiae of the everyday can 'stretch the moral sense of the possible' (Hawkins 2006: 90).[16]

While such accounts are very different, there is much that can be gained from bringing them together, as they both share a critique of Anglo-American government for not implementing green enough policies and together can be used to create a much more nuanced interpretation of contemporary green consumption. For while examinations of the micropolitical are richly suggestive of the *range* of potential interactions with green consumption, accounts of the new green order enable us to highlight how environmental change is not simply down to the personalized whims of the individual-as-sovereign-consumer, but rather the types of larger social and cultural organization that might enable them to act – or not – in particular ways. One implication is that we need to put issues of recycling, green consumption and consuming less that cannot be addressed effectively by an individual or family unit higher up on the discursive and political agenda. For instance, household recycling is only a fraction of all recycling (bars, hospitals, restaurants and factories, for example, all having a vast impact); and similarly, procurement policies by schools, hospitals and local government have large purchasing potential for the buying of ethical products.[17] Linking these social, mental and environmental ecologies together, on both a small and large scale, can facilitate an understanding of the political uses that the 'mental ecologies' of individual consumers are being oriented towards, combined with the shape of wider 'social ecologies' that we both inherit and create. By connecting accounts of the micropolitics of desire with those of broader social, environmental and political shifts, and by considering the constant mutations between them, we can only gain a better understanding of, and interaction with, the ecologies of green consumption being created.

Notes

1 Sanctimonious shopping? Ethical consumption as a 'crisis of moralism'

1   I have discussed this formulation elsewhere in relation to gender and con-sumption: see Littler 2008.

2   Such approaches can be mapped onto the side of moral philosophy which has traditionally been less concerned with 'obligation' and more with ideas of 'the good' (Singer 1994). As Nick Couldry puts it, in the process of locating his own work on the ethics of media studies, 'the distinction between approaches to morality based on a notion of the good (ethics, virtue) and those based on a notion of the 'right' (duty, deontology) has been a fundamental fault line in contemporary moral philosophy' (Couldry 2006: 112).

3   'Both 'ethics' and 'morality' have their roots in a word for 'customs', the former being a derivative of the Greek term from which we get 'ethos', and the latter from the Latin root that gives us 'mores', a word still used some-times to describe the customs of a people (Singer 1994: 5). 'Ethikos' is the Ancient Greek word meaning 'arising from habit'.

4   Foucault's work, for example, was to translate Nietzsche's infatuation with the aristocracy and concomitant ideas of exploitation as a life-source into a less reified template which could imagine power as being everywhere, exploitation as a mutually construed phenomena, and morality – now transmuted into its different incarnation as ethics – as a more radically con-tingent set of practices. Although, arguably, what gets lost in Foucault is the concern with the kind of questions the term 'morality' lets writers such as Bauman ask; and to some extent it is mainly Foucault's post-Marxist sensi-bility, rather than anything particular to his theory of ethics, which means his work escapes the downsides of Nietzschian morality theory (or the potential problems of what Keith Ansell-Pearson terms his 'anarchic hedonism' (Ansell-Pearson 1994)).

5   'The new ethical avant-garde urges a morality of pleasure as duty. This doc-trine makes it a failure, a threat to self-esteem, not to 'have fun', or, as Par-isians like to say with a little shudder of audacity, *jouir*; pleasure is not only permitted but demanded, on ethical as much as on scientific grounds. The fear of not getting enough pleasure, the logical outcome of the effort to overcome the fear of pleasure, is combined with the search for self-expression and 'bodily expression', and for communication with others ('relating' – exchange) even immersion in others (considered not as a group but as

subjectivities in search of their identity); and the old personal ethics is thus rejected for a cult of personal health and psychological therapy (Bourdieu 1979/1986: 367).

Cosmopolitan caring: globalization, charity and the activist-consumer

1 http://www.americanexpress.com/pes/uk/benefits/red/microsite/features.shtml. Accessed March 2007.

2 This often used to be perceived as symbolized by the tenured, jet-setting academic, although in itself this is a marker of those headily social democratic days when there was more job security and money in universities.

3 Brennan also discusses Gramsci's interest in 'imperial cosmopolitanism' as an idealistic detour from internationalist solidarity.

4 http://www.americanexpress.com/pes/uk/benefits/red/microsite/features.shtml. Accessed March 2007.

5 http://www.americanexpress.com/pes/uk/benefits/red/microsite/features.shtml. Accessed March 2007.

6 'The Most Powerful Brands 2006', *Business Week*/Interbrand. http://bwnt. businessweek.com/brand/2006/. Accessed March 2007.

7 'Financialization' gestures towards the process through which a 'shark-like financial services industry' has become extraordinarily rich by expanding through a number of genre-busting techniques (derivatives, swaps, hedge funds, micro-finance, expanded consumer credit and asset-stripping) that even journals like *The Economist* find 'mind-boggling' in their implications (Blackburn 2006: 39). In this world of 'post-monopoly capitalism', not only are commodities as goods traded, or, we might add, cultural services and experience, but increasingly, finance itself: 'personal debt, mortgages of every types, currency contracts, corporate securities and variance swaps' (2006: 69).

8 http://www.mecca-cola.com/. Also quoted in http://en.wikipedia.org/wiki/ Mecca_Cola. Accessed February 2007.

9 As Peter Gowan puts it, since the Clinton and particularly the Bush administration, a liberal cosmopolitan discourse of being 'beyond' national self-interest has been increasingly used which in fact serves to justify it; in which 'free trade and liberal democracy' as presented as conditions for cosmopolitan peace while advancing US power and prosperity (Gowan 2003: 53).

10 Interestingly, the words 'boycott' and 'strike' have a very interwoven etymology: while today we associate the former with consumption and the latter with production, they were initially much more connected: 'boycott' as a word derives from the action of workers, and 'strike' was a word applied to consumer behaviour (i.e. abstention) in the 1900s (Micheletti 2003: 38).

11 Mecca Cola's dominance at social forums and the anti-war demo is based on

my own observation; but also see http://en.wikipedia.org/wiki/February_ 15,_2003_anti-war_protest#_note-stwbook. For Mathlouthi discussing his ambitions for Mecca Cola to branch into Latin America, see Eva Cahen, 'Soft drink politics: Mecca Cola takes off in France'. Available at: http://www. cnsnews.com/ViewForeignBureaus.asp?Page=%5CForeignBureaus%5 Carchive% 5C200304%5CFOR20030430e.html.

12 http://zaytoun.org/. Accessed March 2007.
13 See Moor (2003) for a discussion of the broader context of such branding techniques.
14 See http://www.oxfam.org.uk. Accessed May 2005.
15 For a discussion of the international slippages and use of these terms, see Sargeant (2004: 3–25).
16 Varul ends up by arguing, however, that in conjuring up the ghost of colonialism it does us all a service that we need to find ways of moving beyond.
17 Cheah also gestures towards the problems over international aid agencies 'erod[ing] the ability of these already weakened states to implement genuine social redistribution' by taking over some social services from the public sector (Cheah 1998: 31).
18 One key precursor was the Trade Justice Movement. See http://www.tjm. org.uk. Accessed March 2007.

3 Greenwash, whitewash, hogwash? CSR and the media management of consumer concern

1 The rally was held in June 2006 and organized by the CORE coalition and the Trade Justice Movement. See http://www.corporate-responsibility.org/C2B/ document_tree/ViewADocument.asp?ID=107&CatID=33
2 Gap joined the ETI in 2004. The ETI is a UK-based non-profit alliance (founded in 1998) of companies, unions and NGOs working to 'promote and improve corporate codes of practice'. Critics such as Doane (2003a) argue that while the ETI was a useful forum when it was established, it endorsed voluntarism too strongly, fails to rebuke corporate exploitation and so has become used by corporations as a badge of ethical honour which might show selective progress but also masks exploitation. Meanwhile, allegations of the use of forced child labour in the manufacture of GAP clothing once again surfaced in 2007; see, for example, Dugan (2007) Gap launches inquiry into child labour claims, *The Independent*, 29 October 2007. Available at http:// www.independent.co.uk/news/world/americas/gap-launches-inquiry-into-child-labour-claims-395474.html
3 For one good insight into this range of activity, see the CSR online newsletter, CSRwire. http://www.csrwire.com/
4 Interestingly, he also cites the nineteenth-century Co-operative Movement

and the Quakers (neither of which were corporate – rather, socialist) as part of this tradition, indicating something of the way corporate discourse borrows from/co-opts its opposition.

5 Key campaigners over the 2006 Companies Act.

6 And indeed cultural studies-oriented work analysing the work of NGOs has on the whole been conspicuous through its absence.

7 To rehearse what is by now a familiar story, the emergence of post-Fordism from the 1970s in the West marked a significant shift towards consumer-led cultures of production that sought to identify consumer desires (based increasingly on lifestyle rather than on crude class segmentation). By mobilizing such technological advancements in communication, transport and manufacturing, post-Fordism quickly produced short runs of goods to meet and market such perceived consumer needs through extensive branding around 'emotional selling points' expressed through multiple spaces rather than the 'unique selling points' conducted through a more limited range of demarcated advertising channels symptomatic of the produce-now, market-later patterns of Fordism.

8 'Subset' practices of CSR, such as cause-related marketing – as we saw with product RED in the previous chapter – also use synergistic promotional forms typical of post-Fordism, in that they attempt to build effective and *affective* brand associations and to develop forms of cross-promotion (e.g. Tesco's 'computers for schools' campaign) to reach more markets more deeply.

9 For Ulrich Beck, 'the risk society' gestures both to how, in post-Fordist neo-liberal cultures, the individual comes to shoulder more personal responsibility and risk (as the safety net of welfare has been pulled from underneath us like a rug) and to how corporations generate and attempt to manage such risk.

10 http://www.bitc.org.uk/what_we_do/awards_for_excellence/case_studies/index. html. The award is for 'promoting diversity' by employing more Portuguese staff in Britain.

11 'Careers: Why BP?' on the BP website. http://www.bp.com/sectiongeneric article.do?categoryId=9009143&contentId=7017227. Accessed January 2008.

12 The phrase 'prosumer' was initially coined by futurologist Alvin Toffler; see Toffler (1980).

13 It is tempting to turn here to the philosophy of Emmanuel Levinas, whose conception of 'infinite responsibility' has provided a variety of activist/academics with sustenance (e.g. Zylinska 2005) and in this case appears to be a useful way of expanding the notion of responsibility outwards (although, as Stella Sandford and Simon Critchley have both pointed out, Levinas' theories are uncomfortably wedded to the transcendental; Levinas 1969; Sandford 2000; Critchley 2007).

4 Interior economies: anti-consumer activism and the limits of reflexivity

1   In *The Conquest of Cool* (1997), Thomas Frank both flags up what he calls 'the co-optation thesis' and begins to complicate it by locating the symbols of corporate 'co-optation' discourse in the broader context of the cultural turn: 'with products specifically targeted to young people, hip consumerism was a more complex phenomenon than "co-optation" would imply, a larger shift in the values of business culture than a momentarily expedient dalliance with the rebel doings of the young' (Frank 1997: 10: 163). This is mainly drama-tized through his historical case studies rather than theorized with reference to cultural studies theory, as Frank primarily rails against the populism of 'cultural studies' rather than drawing on more radical elements used in cul-tural studies critique (such as the work of Paul du Gay, David Harvey or Scott Lash) with which his work is in many ways actually very compatible.

2   Rebecca Goldstein's phrase comes from her novel, *The Mind-Body Problem*. The map is used to describe what investments one particular character values most – here, in terms of people. The 'mattering map' becomes a way of defining different subjective investments ('I've been trying ... to see the map for what it is: a description of our subjectivity and nothing more' (Goldstein 1985: 173).

3   I am grateful to Roz Galtz for bringing this home to me (Galtz 2004).

4   It could be argued that there needs to be a multi-faceted approach towards constructing consumer alternatives, including approaches which attempt to articulate some of the principles of co-operation to more mainstream dis-courses such as liberal feminist sentiment. This is a valid point. Equally, it is important not to let such problematic discourse colonize the discourse of anti-consumption.

5   For a critique of 'hairshirt' consumption, framed in terms of UK policy recommendations, see Levett (2003).

6   See http://www.buynothingday.co.uk (accessed February 2007).

7   Talen's text is not as primarily 'informational' as *No Logo*, as reflected in the very different publishing profiles for and sales of the books; and in some senses Reverend Billy and the Church of Stop Shopping's main and widest impact is through reportage about the activities in question through jour-nalistic commentary (as the book is primarily for fans and academics).

8   Clearly there are arguments across the spectrum; arguments which perhaps are to some extent incommensurable. I am most persuaded by not insisting logocentrically on one single methodological position but rather to attempt to encourage a variety of approaches to producing critiques. In Lash's terms, this is 'the modesty of the "and", of what Deleuze calls "the conjunction"' (Lash 2002: xii), the implication of which is to attempt to make useful articulations between them.

5 Ecologies of green consumption

1   In Britain, from where I write, changes in the climate are already beginning to graphically alter and reinforce signifiers of national identity: for example, the conservative tabloid *The Daily Mail* runs features about how 'traditional' British countryside flowers are dying out and tropical plants are 'in'; left-liberal broadsheet *The Guardian* describes how a tea plantation has been set up in Cornwall and the empire has (again) come home (Morris 2005).

2   Monbiot's detailed account of the denial industry explores at length how Exxon and Philip Morris in particular conducted an extensive amount of work producing subsidiary organizations that looked 'separate' from their main business, and as if produced by grassroots activists, to deny climate change. A wide range of media organizations took such organizations seriously, from the BBC to CNN. While their influence has waned in Europe, they remain taken seriously in much of the USA and Australia.

3   Although Sarkozy's push for a UN-led international body clashed with Bush's push for a US-led international body. Sarkozy argued that the 20 industrialized countries producing the most greenhouse gas emissions needed to act, 'in particular' the USA followed by China, India, Russia and Brazil (Tisdall 2007).

4   Castree suggests that environmentalism today needs to do several things: to access party-political power more directly (and cultivate the charisma of potential 'leaders'); to 'get over the message that environmentalism is about more than a thing called "the environment"', adopt a more inspiring message, and increase media discussion of actual potential futures; and to avoid separatism (he suggests that some NGOs might merge).

5   While neo-governmentality theory can provide a useful tool for understanding the regulatory flows of contemporary social formations through the desires of individuals, they can also provide us with a somewhat over-rigid framework that does not have the same engagement with questions of power and agency that Foucault had (see Grossberg *et al.* 2003; Couldry and Littler 2008).

6   The television documentary *World in Action* showed the stunted organs of rats fed GM potatoes, and the British press exploded with stories about 'Frankenstein Food'.

7   The most explicit linkage I have found is the astute comment made by Arron Gare: 'although Guattari is the only poststructuralist to have fully embraced the environmental movements, he has shown that poststructuralist postmodernism is implicitly a form of deep ecology' (Gare 2000: 201). Gare was writing in 2000 and so does not mention *The Three Ecologies*, translated in 2002.

8   Not only in terms of class, but also in the sense that the vast majority of the

shoppers were white while the vast majority of people working on the tills were black. Liz Moor and I have explored elsewhere how another example of a large corporate take on 'ethical business', the clothing company American Apparel, can also work to perpetuate and ramify social and cultural forms of segregation through paternalism, union-busting and hierarchization, while it makes promotional capital out of its minimum wage and employee perks (Littler and Moor 2008).

9   Obviously this also raises the issue of which groups can afford the initial outlay, and questions of cultural ease with the conception of re-usability and 'respectability'.

10   Other pastiches included bags proclaiming 'I'm not a douche bag' ('Pick up one here and let everybody know what you already know'). http://fashion indie.com/events/2007/05/09/im-not-a-smug-twat-either/; http://www.fashion indie.com/events/category/green-indie/. The traders were out on Oxford Street in August 2007.

11   See, for example: http://www.thisismoney.co.uk/news/article.html?in_article_ id=419792&in_page_id=2 For the anti-green lobby, for example, such con-tradictions can be used to perpetuate the status quo rather than to seek to address them.

12   Although for one of several critiques of Maslow in the context of consump-tion, see Campbell (1987: 45).

13   See http://www.realsimple.com.

14   Similarly, a 2007 project by the UK Photographer's Gallery, *Plastic Bag Gallery*, invited people to send in their photos of random blue plastic bags. See http:// www.photonet.org.uk/plasticbag/.

15   One example is provided by Lisa Parks's account of trying to find a place to recycle her old computer in California. She drives around trying to find the right place in which it can be dumped and reused: a perfect illustration of the difficulty inherent for so many people in simply gaining access to recycling facilities, the individualistic 'responsibilization' of the process, and the inef-ficient use of resources when people have to go out of their way to find them (Parks 2007: 37–8).

16   Hawkins is here drawing on the work of Jane Bennett (2001) in *The Enchantment of Modern Life*. Princeton, NJ: Princeton University Press.

17   As Barnett *et al.* (2005: 5–6) have shown with their work on fair trade towns.

References

Abbott, J. and Ackbar, M. (dirs) (2003) *The Corporation*. Big Picture Media.

Adbusters (2006) www.blackspotsneaker.org and www.adbusters.org (accessed May 2006).

Aidi, H. (2003) Let us be Moors: Islam, race and connected histories, *Middle East Report* 229, http://www.merip.org/mer/mer229/229_aidi.html (accessed May 2007).

Amin, A. and Thrift, N. (eds) (2004) *The Cultural Economy Reader*. Oxford: Blackwell.

Andrejevic, M. (2004) *Reality TV: The Work of Being Watched*. Langham, MD: Rowman and Littlefield.

Ansell-Pearson, K. (1994) *An Introduction to Nietzsche as Political Thinker*. Cambridge: Cambridge University Press.

Appadurai, A. (1986) *The Social Life of Things: Commodities in Cultural Perspective*. Cambridge: Cambridge University Press.

Appadurai, A. (1996) *Modernity at Large: Cultural Dimensions of Globalization*. Minneapolis: University of Minnesota Press.

Archibugi, D. (ed.) (2003) *Debating Cosmopolitics*. London: Verso.

Arvidsson, A. (2005) *Brands: Meaning and Value in Media Culture*. London: Routledge.

Bakan, J. (2004) *The Corporation*. London: Constable.

Barber, B. (2003) *Jihad vs. McWorld: Terrorism's Challenge to Democracy*. London: Corgi.

Barber, B. (2007) *Consumed*. London: W. W. Norton.

Barner, M. (2007) Be a socially responsible corporation, *Harvard Business Review*, 85(7/8): 59–60.

Barnett, C., Clarke, N., Cloke, P. and Malpass, A. (2004) Articulating ethics and consumption, Cultures of Consumption Working Paper No. 17, London, Birkbeck.

Barnett, C., Clarke, N., Cloke, P. and Malpass, A. (2005) The political ethics of consumerism, *Consumer Policy Review* 15(2): 2–8.

Barnett, C., Clarke, N., Cloke, P. and Malpass, A. (2006) Faith in ethical consumption, unpublished paper.

Barnett, C., Clarke, N., Cloke, P. and Malpass, A. (2007) Globalising the consumer: doing politics in an ethical register, *Political Geography*, 26: 231–49.

Barnett, C. and Soper, K. (2005) Consumers: agents of change?, interview by J. Littler for *Soundings: A Journal of Politics and Culture*, 31: 147–60.

Barratt Brown, M. (1993) *Fairtrade: Reform and Realities in the International Trading System*. London: Zed Books.

Bauman, Z. (1993) *Postmodern Ethics*. Oxford: Blackwell.

Bauman, Z. (1995) *Life in Fragments: Essays in Postmodern Morality*. Oxford: Blackwell.

Bauman, Z. (2000) *The Individualized Society*. London: Sage.

Bayat, A. (2003) The street and the politics of dissent in the Arab world, Middle East Report 226, Spring. Available at: http://www.merip.org/mer/mer226/226_bayat.html (accessed December 2007).

BBC (2005) Recycling around the world. Available at: http://news.bbc.co.uk/1/hi/world/europe/4620041.stm (accessed December 2006).

BBC2 (2004) *Message in a Bottle*. Programme broadcast, 22 February.

Beck, U. (1994) *Risk Society: Towards a New Modernity*. London: Sage.

Beck, U. (2002) The cosmopolitan society and its enemies, *Theory, Culture & Society*, 19(1–2): 17–44.

Beck, U. (2006) *Cosmopolitan Vision*, trans. Ciaran Cronin. Cambridge: Polity.

Beck, U., Giddens, A. and Lash, S. (1994) *Reflexive Modernisation*. Cambridge: Polity.

Belk, R., with Ger, G. and Askegaard, S. (2003) The fire of desire: a multi-sited inquiry into consumer passion, *Journal of Consumer Research*, 30(3): 326–51.

Bell, D. and Valentine, G. (eds) (1997) *Consuming Geographies*. London: Routledge.

Bevan, J. (2001) *The Rise and Fall of Marks and Spencer*. London: Profile Books.

Binkley, S. (2003) The seers of Menlo Park: the discourse of heroic consumption in the Whole Earth Catalog, *Journal of Consumer Culture*, 3(3): 283–313.

Black, M. (1992) *A Cause for Our Times – Oxfam: The First 50 Years*. Oxford: Oxfam/Oxford University Press.

Blackburn, R. (2003) The imperial presidency and the revolutions of modernity, in D. Archibugi (ed.) *Debating Cosmopolitics*. London: Verso, pp. 141–83.

Blackburn, R. (2006) Finance and the fourth dimension, *New Left Review*, 39: 39–70.

Blackmore, S. (2000) *The Meme Machine*. Oxford: Oxford University Press.

Bocock, R. (1993) *Consumption*. London: Routledge.

Boltanski, L. (1999) *Distant Suffering: Politics, Morality and the Media*. Cambridge: Cambridge University Press.

Boltanski, L. and Chiapello, E. (2006) *The New Spirit of Capitalism*. London: Verso.

Bordwell, M. (2002) Jamming culture: Adbuster's hip media campaign against consumerism, in T. Princen, M. Maniates and K. Conca (eds) *Confronting Consumption*, Cambridge, MA: MIT Press.

Bosshart, D. (2006) *Cheap: The Real Cost of the Global Trend for Bargains, Discounts and Consumer Choice*. London: Kogan Page.

Bourdieu, P. ([1979] 1986) *Distinction*. Oxford: Blackwell.

Bourdieu, P. and Wacquant, L. J. D. (1992) *An Invitation to Reflexive Sociology*. Cambridge: Polity.

Bové, J. and Dufour, F. (2001) *The World Is Not for Sale: Farmers Against Junk Food*. London: Verso.

Bowlby, R. (1993) *Shopping with Freud*. London: Routledge.

Boykoff, M. and Goodman, M. (2008) Conspicuous redemption: promises and perils of celebrity involvement in climate change, *Geoforum*, forthcoming.

Brah, A. and Coombes, A. E. (2000) *Hybridity and its Discontents: Politics, Science, Culture*. London: Routledge.

Branston, G. (2007) The planet at the end of the world: 'Event' cinema and the representability of climate change, *New Review of Film and Television Studies*, 5(2): 211–29.

Bratich, J. Z., Packer, J. and McCarthy, C. (eds) (2003) *Foucault, Cultural Studies and Governmentality*. New York: SUNY.

Brennan, T. (2003) Cosmopolitanism and internationalism, in D. Archibugi (ed.) *Debating Cosmopolitics*. London: Verso.

Brierley, S. (2002) *The Advertising Handbook*. London: Routledge.

Brooks, D. (2000) *Bobos in Paradise: The New Upper Class and How They Got There*. New York: Simon and Schuster.

Brown, P. (2004) Monsanto abandons worldwide GM wheat project, *The Guardian*, 11 May. Available at: http://www.guardian.co.uk/society/2004/may/11/environment.gm (accessed January 2007).

Brown, W. (1995) *States of Injury: Power and Freedom in Late Modernity*. Princeton, NJ: Princeton University Press.

Brown, W. (2001) *Politics Out of History*. Princeton, NJ: Princeton University Press.

Brown, W. (2005) *Edgework: Critical Essays on Knowledge and Politics*. Princeton, NJ: Princeton University Press.

Brown, W. (2006) *Regulating Aversion: Tolerance in the Age of Identity*. Princeton, NJ: Princeton University Press.

Bruce, I. (2005) *Charity Marketing: Meeting Need through Customer Focus*. London: ICSA Publishing.

Butler, J. (2004) *Precarious Life: The Power of Mourning and Violence*. London: Verso.

Campbell, C. (1987) *The Romantic Ethic and the Spirit of Modern Consumerism*. Oxford: Blackwell.

Campbell, C. J. (2006) The dawn of the second half of the age of oil, *Soundings*, 34: 56–66.

Carter, E. (1997) *How German Is She? Postwar West German Construction and the Consuming Woman*. Ann Arbor, MI: University of Michigan Press.

Castells, M. (1996) *The Rise of the Network Society*. Oxford: Blackwell.

Castree, N. (2005) *Nature*. London: Routledge.

Castree, N. (2006) The future of environmentalism, *Soundings*, 34: 11–21.

Charities Aid Foundation (2004) The business benefits of CCI. Available at: www.cafonline.org/default.aspx?Page=7923 (accessed December 2007).

Cheah, P. (1998) The cosmopolitical – today, in Pheng Cheah and Bruce Robbins (eds) *Cosmopolitics: Thinking and Feeling Beyond the Nation*. Minneapolis: University of Minnesota Press.

Cheah, P. and Robbins, B. (eds) (1998) *Cosmopolitics: Thinking and Feeling beyond the Nation*. Minneapolis: University of Minnesota Press.

Chouliarki, L. (2006) *The Spectatorship of Suffering*. London: Sage.

Christian Aid (2004) *Behind the Mask: The Real Face of Corporate Social Responsibility*. London: Christian Aid.

Clark, A. (2006) Is Wal-Mart really going green? *The Guardian*, 6 November. Available at: http://www.guardian.co.uk/environment/2006/nov/06/energy. supermarkets (accessed December 2006).

Clark, M. (1994) Nietzsche's immoralism and the concept of morality, in R. Schacht (ed.) *Nietzsche, Genealogy, Morality: Essays on Nietzsche's on the Genealogy of Morals*. Berkeley, CA: University of California Press.

Clifford, J. (1988) *The Predicament of Culture*. Cambridge, MA: Harvard University Press.

Clifford, J. (1998) Mixed feelings, in Pheng Cheah and Bruce Robbins (eds) *Cosmopolitics: Thinking and Feeling Beyond the Nation*. Minneapolis: University of Minnesota Press.

Cohen, L. (2003) *A Consumers' Republic: The Politics of Mass Consumption in Postwar America*. New York: Vintage.

Collard, J. (2005) Too sexy for his shirt, *The Times*, 12 February. Available at: http://www.americanapparel.net/presscenter/articles/20050212thetimesmag. html (accessed July 2006).

Co-operative Bank/New Economics Foundation (2003) *Ethical Purchasing Index 2002*. London: Co-operative Bank/New Economics Foundation.

Couldry, N. (2006) *Listening beyond the Echoes: Media, Ethics and Agency in an Uncertain World*. Boulder, CO: Paradigm Press.

Couldry, N. and Curran, J. (eds) (2003) *Contesting Media Power: Alternative Media in a Networked World*. Lanham, MD: Rowman and Littlefield.

Couldry, N. and Littler, J. (2008) Work, power and performance: analysing the 'reality' game of The Apprentice, *Cultural Sociology*, forthcoming.

Critchley, S. (2007) *Infinitely Demanding: Ethics of Commitment, Politics of Resistance*. London: Verso.

Crocker, D. A. and Linden, T. (1998) *Ethics of Consumption: The Good Life, Justice and Global Stewardship*. Lanham, MD: Rowman and Littlefield.

Daum, M. (2003) *The Quality of Life Report*. New York: Penguin.

Davis, A. (2005) Placing promotional culture, in J. Curran and D. Morley (eds) *Media and Cultural Theory*. London: Routledge.

Davis, M. (2006) Fear and money in Dubai, *New Left Review*, 2(1): 47–68.

Dawkins, R. (1989) *The Selfish Gene*. Oxford: Oxford University Press.

Debord, G. ([1967] 1994) *The Society of the Spectacle*. New York: Zone Books.

de Graaf, J., Wann, D. and Naylor, T. H. (2005) *Affluenza: The All-Consuming Epidemic*. San Francisco: Berrett Koehler.

de Jong, M., Shaw, P. and Stammers, N. (eds) (2005) *Global Activism, Global Media*. London: Pluto Press.

Deleuze, G. (1995) *Negotiations 1972–1990*. New York: Columbia University Press.

Deleuze, G. and Guattari, F. ([1972] 1992) *Anti-Oedipus: Capitalism and Schizophrenia*, trans. R. Hurley, M. Seem and H. R. Lane. Minneapolis: University of Minnesota Press.

Deleuze, G. and Guattari, F. ([1972] 2004) *Anti-Oedipus*. London: Continuum.

Deleuze, G. and Guattari, F. ([1980] 2004) *A Thousand Plateaus*. London: Continuum.

Derrida, J. (2001) *On Cosmopolitanism and Forgiveness*. London: Routledge.

Doane, D. (2003a) Commentary and analysis: CSR, *International Journal of Corporate Sustainability*, 10(2): 4–7.

Doane, D. (2003b) Married to the mob, *Open Democracy*. Available at: http://www.opendemocracy.net/theme_7–corporations/article_1121.jsp (accessed March 2007).

Doane, D. (2004) Good intentions – bad outcomes? The broken promise of CSR reporting, in A. Henriques and J. Richardson (eds) *The Triple Bottom Line: Does It All Add Up? – Assessing the Sustainability of Business and CSR*. London: Earthscan.

Dollimore, J. (2001) *Sex, Literature and Censorship*. Cambridge: Polity.

Dugan, E. (2007) Gap launches inquiry into child labour claims, *The Independent*, 29 October 2007. Available at http://www.independent.co.uk/news/world/americas/gap-launches-inquiry-into-child-labour-claims-395474.html (accessed December 2007).

du Gay, P. (ed.) (1997) *Production of Culture/Cultures of Production*. London: Sage.

du Gay, P. and Pryke, M. (eds) (2002) *Cultural Economy*. London: Sage.

Duncan, C. (1995) *Civilizing Rituals*. London: Routledge.

Elgin, D. (1981) *Voluntary Simplicity: Toward a Way of Life that Is Outwardly Simple*. New York: Morrow & Co.

Emmerich, R. (dir) (2004) *The Day After Tomorrow*. Twentieth Century Fox.

Fairtrade Foundation (2003) *Fairtrade Highlights 2002: Annual Report*. London: Fairtrade Foundation.

Fairtrade Foundation (2007) 7 million farming families worldwide benefit as global fairtrade sales increase by 40%, Press Release. http://www.fairtrade.org.uk/press_office/press_releases_and_statements/archive_2007/aug_2007/global_fairtrade_sales_increase_by_40_benefiting_14_million_farmers_worldwide.aspx (accessed January 2008).

Farquarson, A. (2000) Marketing campaigns impact on consumer habits, *The Guardian*, 15 November. Available at: http://www.guardian.co.uk/society/2000/nov/15/voluntarysector.fundraising (accessed March 2007).

Featherstone, L. (2005) *Selling Women Short: The Landmark Battle for Workers' Rights at Wal-Mart.* New York: Basic Books.

Featherstone, M. (1991) *Consumer Culture and Postmodernism.* London: Sage.

Featherstone, M. (2002) Cosmopolis: an introduction, *Theory, Culture & Society,* Special Issue on 'Cosmopolis', 19(1–2): 1–6.

Finkelpearl, T. (2001) Interview: Mierle Laderman Ukeles on maintenance and sanitation art, in *Dialogues in Public Art.* Cambridge, MA: MIT Press.

Foley, J. (2006) *Zero Waste UK.* London: IPPR.

Foot, P. (1994) Nietzsche's immoralism, in Richard Schacht (ed.) *Nietzsche, Genealogy, Morality: Essays on Nietzsche's On the Genealogy of Morals.* Berkeley, CA: University of California Press.

Forsyth, T. and Young, Z. (2007) Climate change Co$_2$lonialism, *MUTE,* 2(5): 28–35.

Foucault, M. (1982) The subject and power, in H. Dreyfus and P. Rabinow (eds) *Michel Foucault: Beyond Structuralism and Hermeneutics.* Chicago: University of Chicago Press.

Foucault, M. ([1983] 2003) On the genealogy of ethics, interview with H. Dreyfus and P. Rabinow, in M. Calarco and P. Atterton (eds) *The Continental Ethics Reader.* London: Routledge.

Foucault, M. (1986) *The History of Sexuality* Vol. Three: *The Care of the Self.* London: Penguin.

Frank, T. (1997) *The Conquest of Cool: Business Culture, Counterculture and the Rise of Hip Consumerism.* Chicago: University of Chicago Press.

Friedman, M. (1970) The social responsibility of business is to increase its profits, *New York Times Magazine,* 13 September. Online at: http://www.colorado.edu/studentgroups/libertarians/issues/friedman-soc-resp-business.html (accessed March 2007).

Fukuyama, F. (1992) *The End of History and the Last Man.* New York: Free Press.

Gabriel, Y. and Lang, T. (1995) *The Unmanageable Consumer: Contemporary Consumption and its Fragmentations.* London: Sage.

Galtz, R. (2004) Consumption at the brink: the radically simplified spaces of *Fight Club* and *Matrix 2,* paper delivered at *Crossroads in Cultural Studies* Conference.

Gare, A. (2000) The postmodernism of deep ecology, the deep ecology of postmodernsim, and grand narratives, in E. Katz, A. Light and D. Rothenberg (eds) *Beneath the Surface: Critical Essays in the Philosophy of Deep Ecology.* Cambridge, MA: MIT Press.

Gauntlett, D. (2002) *Media, Gender and Identity.* London: Routledge.

Genette, G. (1997) *Paratexts: Thresholds of Interpretation,* trans. J. E. Lewin. Cambridge: Cambridge University Press.

Genosko, G. (2002) *Félix Guattari: An Aberrant Introduction.* London: Continuum.

Giddens, A. (1991) *Modernity and Self-Identity: Self and Society in the Late Modern Age.* London: Polity.

Gilbert, J. (2008) Beyond the activist imaginary, in *Anti-Capitalism and Culture: Radical Theory and Popular Politics*. Oxford: Berg.

Gilroy, P. (2000) *Between Camps: Nations, Cultures and the Allure of Race*. London: Penguin.

Glyn, A. (2006) *Capitalism Unleashed*. Oxford: Oxford University Press.

Goff, S. (2007) Inheritance is child's play, *FT Report: Wealth Quarterly*, 23 March. Online at http://www.ft.com (accessed November 2007).

Goldblatt, D. (ed.) (2000) *Knowledge and the Social Sciences*. London: Routledge.

Goldstein, R. (1985) *The Mind-Body Problem*. New York: Penguin.

Gopal, P. (2006) The 'moral empire': Africa, globalisation and the politics of conscience, *New Formations*, 59: 81–97.

Gowan, P. (2003) The new liberal cosmopolitanism, in D. Archibugi (ed.) *Debating Cosmopolitics*. London: Verso.

Gramsci, A. ([1934] 1988) Americanism and Fordism, in D. Forgacs (ed.) *A Gramsci Reader*. London: Lawrence & Wishart.

Gregg, M. and Seigworth, G. (forthcoming) *The Affect Reader*. Durham, NC: Duke University Press.

Gregson, N. and Crewe, L. (2003) *Second-Hand Cultures*. Oxford: Berg.

Grossberg, L. (1992) *We Gotta Get Out of This Place: Popular Conservatism and Postmodern Culture*. London: Routledge.

Grossberg, L. (1997) *Bringing It all Back Home: Essays on Cultural Studies*. Durham, NC: Duke University Press.

Grossberg, L. (2005) *Caught in the Crossfire: Kids, Politics, and America's Future*. Boulder, CO: Paradigm Publishers.

Grossberg, L., Miller, T. and Packer, J. (2003) Interview with Lawrence Grossberg and Toby Miller, in J.Z. Bratich, J. Packer, and C. McCarthy (eds) *Foucault, Cultural Studies and Governmentality*. New York: SUNY.

Grosz, E. (1995) *Space, Time and Perversion*. London: Routledge.

Guattari, F. ([1989] 2000) *The Three Ecologies*, trans. I. Pindar and P. Sutton. London: Continuum.

Guggenheim, D. (dir) (2006) *An Inconvenient Truth*, Paramount Pictures.

Hall, C. (1998) Going a-trolloping, in C. Midgely (ed.) *Gender and Imperialism*. Manchester: Manchester University Press.

Hall, S. (1992) The West and the rest: discourse and power, in S. Hall and B. Gieben (eds) *Formations of Modernity*. London: Polity Press.

Hall, S. (1997) The centrality of culture: notes on the cultural revolutions of our time, in K. Thompson (ed.) *Media and Cultural Regulation*. London: Sage.

Hall, S., Critcher, C., Jefferson, T., Clarke, J. and Robert, B. (1978) (eds) *Policing the Crisis*. London: Palgrave.

Hall, S. and Jacques, M. (eds) (1989) *New Times*. London: Lawrence & Wishart.

Hamilton, C. (2003) *Growth Fetish*. London: Pluto.

Hamilton, C. (2007) Building on Kyoto, *New Left Review*, 45: 91–104.

Hansley, S. (2005) Whose responsibility?, *PR Week*, 12 August, 21–2.

Haraway, D. (1997) *Modest_Witness@Second_Millennium: FemaleMan©_Meets_ OncoMouse™: Feminism and Technoscience*. London: Routledge.

Harding, S. (2003) *The Feminist Standpoint Theory Reader*. London: Routledge.

Hardt, M. (2002) The collective project for a global commons, *New Formations*, 45: 221–2.

Hardt, M. and Negri, A. (2005) *Multitude*. London: Penguin.

Harrison, R., Shaw, D. and Newholm, T. (eds) (2005) *The Ethical Consumer*. London: Sage.

Harvey, D. (1989) *The Condition of Postmodernity*. Oxford: Basil Blackwell.

Harvey, D. (2003) *The New Imperialism*. Oxford: Oxford University Press.

Harvey, D. (2005) *A Brief History of Neoliberalism*. Oxford: Oxford University Press.

Hawkins, G. (2006) *The Ethics of Waste: How We Relate to Rubbish*. Lanham, MD: Rowman and Littlefield.

Hay, J. and Oullette, L. (2008) *Better Living Through Reality TV: Television and Post-Welfare Citizenship*. Hoboken, NJ: John Wiley and Sons.

Haynes, J. and Littler, J. (2007) Documentary as political activism: an interview with Robert Greenwald, *Cineaste* 32(4): 26–9.

HealthWatch (2000) The GM furore: who's to blame? *Healthwatch Newsletter*, No. 36. http://www.healthwatch-uk.org/newsletterarchive/nlett36.html. (accessed January 2008).

Hebdige, D. (1981) *Subculture: The Meaning of Style*. London: Routledge.

Held, D. (2003) Violence, law and justice in a global age, in D. Archibugi (ed.) *Debating Cosmopolitics*. London: Verso.

Heminsley, A. (2007) When Gisele Met Keseme, American Express RED website. http://www.americanexpress.com/pes/uk/benefits/red/microsite/index.shtml (accessed February 2006).

Henderson, D. (2001) *Misguided Virtue*. Hobart Paper, 142. London: IEA.

Henderson, D. (2004) *The Role of Business in the Modern World*. London: CEI.

Hennessey, P. (2006) *Having It So Good: Britain in the Fifties*. London: Penguin.

Henriques, A. (2007) *Corporate Truth: The Limits to Transparency*. London: Earthscan.

Henriques, A. and Richardson, J. (eds) (2004) *The Triple Bottom Line: Does It All Add Up? Assessing the Sustainability of Business and CSR*. London: Earthscan.

Hertz, N. (2001) *The Silent Takeover: Global Capitalism and the Death of Democracy*. London: Heinemann.

Hilton, M. (2003) *Consumerism in Twentieth-Century Britain: The Search for an Historical Movement*. Cambridge: Cambridge University Press.

Hilton, M. (2007) Consumers and the State since the Second World War, *The Annals of the American Academy of Political and Social Science*, 611: 66–81.

Holt, D. and Schor, J. (eds) (2000) *The Consumer Society Reader*. New York: New Press.

hooks, b. (1990) *Yearning: Race, Gender and Cultural Politics*. Boston: South End Press.

hooks, b. (1992) Eating the other: desire and resistance, in *Black Looks: Race and Representation*. Boston: South End Press.

Hopkins, M. (2003) *The Planetary Bargain: Corporate Social Responsibility Matters*, 2nd edn. London: Earthscan.

Hopkins, M. (2007) *Corporate Social Responsibility and International Development: Is Business the Solution?* London: Earthscan.

Huntington, S. (1996) *The Clash of Civilizations and the Remaking of World Order*. New York: Simon and Schuster.

Hutnyk, J. (1996) *The Rumour of Calcutta: Tourism, Poverty and Representation*. London: Zed Books.

Huyssen, A. (1987) *After the Great Divide: Modernism, Mass Culture and Post-modernism*. Bloomington, IN: Indiana University Press.

ICA (2004) CSR: Greenwash or a movement to change capitalism? Debate in the Nash Room, 27 July.

Iggulden, A. (2005) The power of the pink ribbon? *The Telegraph*, 4 April. http://www.telegraph.co.uk/health/main.jhtml?xml=/health/2005/10/04/hpink04.xml (accessed January 2008).

Illouz, E. (2007) *Cold Intimacies: The Making of Emotional Capitalism*. Cambridge: Polity.

IPPR (2006) Britain bottom of the heap for recycling, Press Release, 27 August. http://www.ippr.org.uk/pressreleases/?id=2283 (accessed December 2007).

IPPR and Green Alliance (2006) *A Zero Waste UK*. London: IPPR.

Jackson, T. (ed.) (2007) *The Earthscan Reader in Sustainable Consumption*. London: Earthscan.

James, O. (2007) *Affluenza: How to Be Successful and Stay Sane*. London: Vermillion.

Jamoul, L. (2006) The art of politics: broad-based organising in Britain, PhD thesis, Queen Mary, University of London. Published online by TELCO: http://www.londoncitizens.org.uk/files/LinaJamoulPhD.pdf (accessed June 2007).

Jordan, J. (1998) The art of necessity: the subversive imagination of anti-road protest and Reclaim the Streets, in G. McKay (ed.) *DiY Culture: Party and Protest in Nineties Britain*. London: Verso.

Juniper, T. (2004) *A New Deal*. http://www.bigpicture.tv/videos/watch/93db85ed9 (accessed December 2007).

Kalhar, T. (2008) When Red Pepper met Anita Roddick, Red Pepper. Available at http://www.redpepper.org.uk/article471.html (accessed December 2007).

Kaplan, C. (1999) 'A World without boundaries': The Body Shop's trans/national geographics, in L. Bloom (ed.) *With Other Eyes: Looking at Race and Gender in Visual Culture*. Minneapolis: University of Minnesota Press.

Kastner, J. (2002) The Department of Sanitation's artist in residence, *The New York Times*, 19 May. Reprinted at http://www.feldmangallery.com (accessed July 2007).

Katz, E., Light, A. and Rothenberg, D. (eds) (2000) *Beneath the Surface: Critical Essays in the Philosophy of Deep Ecology*. Cambridge, MA: MIT Press.

Kingsnorth, P. (2003) The Church of Stop Shopping, in *One No, Many Yeses: A Journey to the Heart of the Global Resistance Movement*. London: Free Press.

Klein, N. (2000) *No Logo: Taking Aim at the Brand Bullies*. London: Flamingo.

Klein, N. (2002) *Fences and Windows: Dispatches from the Front Lines of the Globalization Debates*. London: Flamingo.

Kotler, P. and Andreasen, A. (2007) *Strategic Marketing for Nonprofit Organisations*. Englewood Cliffs, NJ: Prentice Hall.

Kotler, P. and Lee, N. (2006) *Corporate Social Responsibility: Doing the Most Good For Your Company and Your Cause*. Hoboken, NJ: John Wiley and Sons.

Krauss, C. (2007) Retailer looks for ways to apply a Green label, *New York Times* extract in *The Observer*, 8 July: 1–2.

Laclau, E. and Mouffe, C. (1985) *Hegemony and Socialist Strategy*. London: Verso.

Laclau, E. and Mouffe, C. (2003) Hope, passion, politics: a conversation with Chantal Mouffe and Ernesto Laclau, in M. Zournazi (ed.) *Hope: New Philosophies for Change*. London: Lawrence & Wishart.

Lash, S. (2002) *Critique of Information*. London: Sage.

Lash, S. and Urry, J. (1994) *Economies of Signs and Space*. London: Sage.

Lasn, K. (1999) *Culture Jam: The Uncooling of America*. New York: Eagle Brook.

Latour, B. (2002) Morality and technology: the end of the means, *Theory, Culture & Society*, 19(5/6): 248–60.

Latour, B. (2004) *Politics of Nature: How to Bring the Sciences into Democracy*. Cambridge, MA: Harvard University Press.

Layard, R. (2006) *Happiness: Lessons from a New Science*. London: Penguin.

Law, J. and Hassard, J. (eds) (1999) *Actor Network Theory and After*. Oxford: Blackwell.

Lawson, N. (2008) *All-Consuming*. London: Penguin, forthcoming.

Lee, M. J. (1993) *Consumer Culture Reborn: The Cultural Politics of Consumption*. London: Routledge.

Levett, R. (2003) *A Better Choice of Choice: Quality of Life, Consumption and Economic Growth*. London: Fabian Society.

Levinas, E. (1969) *Totality and Infinity*. Pittsburgh, PA: Duquense University Press.

Lezaun, J. (2004) Genetically modified foods and consumer mobilization in the UK, *Theorie und Praxis*, 3(13): 49–56. Available at: http://www.itas.fzk.de/tatup/043/leza04a.htm (accessed December 2007).

Littler, J. (2002) Pipe dreamer?, *New Formations*, 45: 206–9.

Littler, J. (2004) Putting the shoe on the other foot: an interview with Kalle Lasn. Available at: www.signsofthetimes.org.uk.

Littler, J. (2005) Beyond the boycott: anti-consumerism, cultural change and the limits of reflexivity, *Cultural Studies*, 19(2): 227–52.

Littler, J. (2007) Celebrity CEOs and the cultural economy of tabloid intimacy, in S. Holmes and S. Redmond (eds) *A Reader in Stardom and Celebrity*. London: Sage.

Littler, J. (2008) Gendering anti-consumerism, in M. Ryle, K. Soper and L. Thomas (eds) *Counter-Consumerism and its Pleasures: Better Than Shopping.* Basingstoke: Palgrave.

Littler, J. and Moor, L. (2008) Fourth worlds and neo-Fordism: American Apparel and the cultural economy of consumer anxiety, *Cultural Studies,* 22(5–6), forthcoming.

Livingston, S. (2003) The vicious virtues of the virtuous brand, *Blueprint,* 14 April. http://www.wolffolins.com/Viciousvirtues.htm (accessed June 2006).

Luke, T. W. (1999) Environmentality as green governmentality, in É. Darier (ed.) *Discourses of the Environment.* Oxford: Blackwell.

Lury, C. (1996) *Consumer Culture.* Cambridge: Polity.

Lury, C. (2004) *Brands: The Logos of the Global Economy.* London: Routledge.

Macguire, K. (2003) How British charity was silenced on Iraq, *The Guardian,* 28 November, http://www.guardian.co.uk/Iraq/Story/0,2763,1095116,00.html (accessed February 2007).

MacPherson, C. B. (1962) *The Political Theory of Possessive Individualism: Hobbes to Locke.* Oxford: Clarendon Press.

Malcolm X, Haley, A. (2001) *The Autobiography of Malcolm X.* London: Penguin.

Maniates, M. (2002) Individualization: plant a tree, buy a bike, save the world?, in T. Princen, M. Maniates and K. Conca (eds) *Confronting Consumption.* Cambridge, MA: MIT Press.

Manzoor, S. (2006) Revelation in (Moto) Red Square. Available at: http://www.americanexpress.com/pes/uk/benefits/red/microsite/features9.shtml (accessed February 2006).

Maslow, A. (1943) A theory of human motivation, *Psychological Review,* 50: 370–96.

Massey, D. (2002) Globalisation as geometries of power, Signs of the Times Discussion Paper 18 October. http://www.signsofthetimes.org.uk (accessed February 2007).

McGuigan, J. (2005) A community of communities, in J. Littler and R. Naidoo (eds) *The Politics of Heritage: The Legacies of 'Race'.* London: Routledge.

McGuigan, J. (2006a) The politics of cultural studies and cool capitalism, *Cultural Politics,* 2(2): 137–58.

McGuigan, J. (2006b) Culture and risk, in G. Mythen and S. Walklate (eds) *Beyond the Risk Society.* Maidenhead: Open University Press.

McKibben, B. (2006) Hype vs. hope: is corporate do-goodery for real? *Mother Jones* November/December. Available at: http://www.motherjones.com/news/feature/2006/11/hype_vs_hope.html (accessed July 2007).

McRobbie, A. (2005) *The Uses of Cultural Studies.* London: Sage.

Mellor, M. (2006) Down to earth economics, *Soundings,* 34: 22–31.

Merck, M. (ed.) (2004) Cultures and economies, *New Formations,* 52.

Mertes, T. (ed.) (2004) *A Movement of Movements: Is Another World Really Possible?* London: Verso.

Micheletti, M. (2003) *Political Virtue and Shopping.* London: Palgrave Macmillan.

Micheletti, M., Follesdal, A. and Stolle, D. (eds) (2004) *Politics, Products and Markets*. New Brunswick, NJ: Transaction.

Milmo, C. (2006) Ethical shopping: the RED revolution, *The Independent*, 27 January. http://news.independent.co.uk/world/politics/article341256.ece (accessed July 2007).

Monbiot, G. (2001) Cause-related marketing is a new form of social control. *The Guardian*, 31 July. Available at: http://www.monbiot.com/archives/2001/07/31/privatising-our-minds/ (accessed March 2007).

Monbiot, G. (2002) Greens get eaten, *The Guardian*, 15 January, available at: http://www.monbiot.com (accessed July 2007).

Monbiot, G. (2007a) *Heat: How We Can Stop the Planet Burning*. London: Penguin.

Monbiot, G. (2007b) Environmental feedback, *New Left Review*, 45: 105–13.

Montague, J. (2007) *Stray Shopping Carts of Eastern North America: A Guide to Field Identification*. New York: Harry N. Abrams.

Moor, L. (2003) Branded spaces: the scope of 'New Marketing', *Journal of Consumer Culture*, 3(1): 39–60.

Moor, L. (2007) *The Rise of Brands*. Oxford: Berg.

Moore, A. E. (2007) *Unmarketable: Brandalism, Copyfighting and the Erosion of Integrity*. New York: The New Press.

Morley, D. (2000) Cosmopolitics, in *Home Territories: Media, Mobility and Identity*. London: Routledge.

Morris, S. (2005) English breakfast teas? Make sure it's grown in Cornwall. *The Guardian*, 20 June. Available at: http://www.guardian.co.uk/food/Story/0,2763,1510364,00.html (accessed March 2007).

Mouffe, C. (2005) *On the Political*. London: Routledge.

Muchhala, B. (2004) Students against sweatshops, in T. Mertes (ed.) *A Movement of Movements: Is Another World Really Possible?* London: Verso.

Murray, R. (1989) Fordism and post-Fordism, in S. Hall and M. Jacques (eds) *New Times*. London: Lawrence & Wishart.

Murray, R. (1999) *Creating Wealth from Waste*. London: DEMOS.

Murray, R. (2007) Discussion at *Soundings* seminar, London, July.

Nancy, J. (1991) *The Inoperative Community*. Minneapolis: University of Minnesota.

Nash, K. (2008) Global citizenship as showbusiness: the cultural politics of Make Poverty History, *Media, Culture and Society*, 30(2): 167–81.

Nava, M. (1992) *Changing Cultures: Feminism, Youth and Consumerism*. London: Sage.

Nava, M. (1996) Modernity's disavowal: women, the city and the department store, in M. Nava and A. O'Shea (eds) *Modern Times*. London: Routledge.

Nava, M., Blake, A., McRury, I. and Richards, B. (1997) Introduction, in *Buy This Book: Studies in Advertising and Consumption*. London: Routledge.

Neff, G. (1996) Microcredit, Microresult, *Left Business Observer*, No. 74. Available at: http://www.leftbusinessobserver.com/Micro.html (accessed March 2007).

Nelson, M. R., Rademacher, M. A. and Paek, H-J. (2007) Downshifting consumer = upshifting citizen? An examination of a local freecycle community, *The Annals of the American Academy of Political and Social Science*, 611: 141–56.

New Economics Foundation (2002) *An Ethical Door Policy*. London: New Economics Foundation.

Nicholls, A. and Opal, C. (2005) *Fair Trade: Market-Driven Ethical Consumption*. London: Sage.

Nietzsche, F. ([1886] 1997) *Beyond Good and Evil: Prelude to a Philosophy of the Future*. New York: Dover Press.

Nietzsche, F. ([1887] 2003) *The Genealogy of Morals*. New York: Dover Press.

Notes from Nowhere (2003) *We Are Everywhere: The Irresistible Rise of Global Anticapitalism*. London: Verso.

Oxfam (2002a) Mugged: poverty in your coffee cup. www.oxfam.org/en/policy/ (accessed March 2005).

Oxfam (2002b) Rigged rules and double standards. www.oxfam.org/en/policy (accessed March 2005).

Oxfam (2004) Report from the World Social Forum, Mumbai, India, 16–21 January. Available at: http://www.maketradefair.com (accessed March 2005).

Packard, V. (1957) *The Hidden Persuaders*. London: Penguin.

Parkins, W. and Craig, G. (2006) *Slow Living*. Oxford: Berg.

Parks, L. (2007) Falling apart: electronics salvaging and the global media economy, in C. Acland (ed.) *Residual Media*. Minneapolis: University of Minnesota Press.

Pine, B. J. and Gilmour, J. H. (1999) *The Experience Economy*. Cambridge, MA: Harvard Business School Press.

Pratt, M. L. (1992) *Imperial Eyes: Travel Writing and Transculturation*. London: Routledge.

Prendergast, M. (1994) *For God, Country and Coca-Cola*. London: Phoenix.

Princen, T., Maniates, M. and Conca, K. (eds) (2002) *Confronting Consumption*. Cambridge, MA: MIT Press.

Quarmby, K. (2005) Why Oxfam is failing Africa, *New Statesman*, 30 May: 10–12.

Quelch, J. and Laider-Kylander, N. (2005) *The New Global Brands: Managing Nongovernmental Organisations in the 21st Century*. Mason, OH: South Western.

Ramamurthy, A. (2003) *Imperial Persuaders: Images of Africa and Asia in British Advertising*. Manchester: Manchester University Press.

Retort (2005) *Afflicted Powers: Capital and Spectacle in a New Age of War*. London: Verso.

Ritzer, G. (2002) Revolutionizing the world of consumption, *Journal of Consumer Culture*, 2(1): 103–18.

Ritzer, G. (ed.) (2006) *McDonaldization: The Reader*. Thousand Oaks, CA: Pine Forge Press.

Robbins, B. (1998) Comparative cosmopolitanisms, in P. Cheah and B. Robbins (eds) *Cosmopolitics: Thinking and Feeling beyond the Nation*. Minneapolis: University of Minnesota Press.

Roddick, A. (2001) *Take it Personally: How Globalisation Affects You and Powerful Ways to Challenge It: An Action Guide for Conscious Consumers*. London: Element.

Rodinson, M. (1974) *Islam and Capitalism*. New York: Pantheon.

Rose, N. (1989) *Governing the Soul: The Shaping of the Private Self.* London: Free Association Books.

Ross, A. (ed.) (1997) *No Sweat: Fashion, Free Trade, and the Rights of Garment Workers*. London: Routledge.

Ross, A. (2006) *Fast Boat to China: High-tech Outsourcing and the Consequences of Free Trade – Lessons from Shanghai*. New York: Vintage.

Ross, A. (2008) The quandaries of consumer-based labor activism: a low-wage case study, *Cultural Studies*, 22(5–6), forthcoming.

Rowbotham, S. (2000) *Promise of a Dream: Remembering the Sixties*. London: Penguin.

Rowell, A. (2005) Did you have a Coke-free Christmas?, *Spinwatch*, 3 January. Available at: http://www.spinwatch.org/content/view/121/8/ (accessed February 2008).

Roy, A. (2004) *The Chequebook and the Cruise Missile*. London: Harper.

Said, E. (2001) The clash of ignorance, *The Nation*, 22 October. Available at http://www.thenation.com/doc/20011022/said (accessed March 2007).

Sandford, S. (2000) *The Metaphysics of Love: Gender and Transcendence in Levinas*. London: Continuum.

Sargeant, A. (2004) *Marketing Management for Nonprofit Organisations*. Oxford: Oxford University Press.

Sassatelli, R. (2007) *Consumer Culture: History, Theory and Politics*. London: Sage.

Save the Children and the Core Coalition (2007) *Why CSR is Failing Children*. London: Save the Children and the Core Coalition.

Scanlan, J. (2005) *On Garbage*. London: Reaktion.

Schlosser, E. (2002) *Fast Food Nation: The Dark Side of the All-American Meal*. London: Penguin.

Schor, J. (2006) Tackling turbo consumption: an interview with Juliet Schor, by J. Littler, *Soundings*, 34: 45–55.

Seyfang, G. (2003) From Frankenstein foods to veggie box schemes: sustainable consumption in cultural perspective, EDM Working Paper 13, University of East Anglia.

Shaw, A. (2002) 'It just goes against the grain': public understandings of geneti-cally modified (GM) food in the UK, *Public Understanding of Science*, 11(3): 273–81.

Shaw, D. and Newholm, T. (2002) Voluntary simplicity and the ethics of consumption, *Psychology and Marketing*. 19(2): 167–85.

Shepard, B. and Hayduk, R. (eds) (2002) *From ACT UP to the WTO: Urban Protest and Community Building in the Era of Globalization*. London: Verso.

Silverman, G. (2006) Amex 'pulls' customers to 'push' its plastic, *Financial Times*, 30 January. Available at: www.ft.com (accessed February 2007).

Simms, A. (2005) *Ecological Debt: The Health of the Planet and the Wealth of Nations*. London: Pluto.

Simms, A. (2007) *Tescopoly: How One Shop Came Out on Top and Why It Matters*. London: Constable.

Singer, P. (ed.) (1994) *Ethics*. Oxford: Oxford University Press.

Slater, D. (1997) *Consumer Culture and Modernity*. Cambridge: Polity.

Smith, A. and Baird, N. (2005) *Save Cash and Save the Planet*. London: Collins/ Friends of the Earth.

Smith, C. (1994a) The new corporate philanthropy, *Harvard Business Review*, 72(3): 105–16.

Smith, C. (1994b) How corporate philanthropy promotes causes, *Harvard Business Review*, 72(3): 106–8.

Smith, M. (2000) On the state of cultural studies: an interview with Paul Gilroy, *Third Text*, 49: 15–26.

Soar, M. (2000) The politics of culture jamming: Adbusters on the web and in print, *M/C reviews*, 12 April. http://www.uq.edu.au/mc/reviews/features/ politics/jamming.html (accessed May 2005).

Soar, M. (2002) The First Things First Manifesto and the politics of culture jamming: towards a cultural economy of graphic design and advertising, *Cultural Studies*, 16(4): 570–92.

Soil Association (2007) *Organic Market Report*. Bristol: Soil Association.

Soper, K. (2008) Alternative hedonism, cultural theory and the role of aesthetic revisioning, *Cultural Studies*, 22(5–6), forthcoming.

Spivak, G. (1998) Cultural talks in the hot peace, in P. Cheah and B. Robbins (eds) *Cosmopolitics: Thinking and Feeling beyond the Nation*. Minneapolis: University of Minnesota Press.

Spotts, G. (2006) *The High Cost of Low Price*. New York: Disinformation Books.

Spurlock, M. (dir) (2004) *Super Size Me*. Kathbur Pictures/Showtime Network.

Stauber, J. and Rampton, S. (1995) *Toxic Sludge is Good for You!* Monroe, ME: Common Courage Press.

Stein, L. (2003) Action Aid's marketing and branding techniques, invited talk given at Middlesex University, London.

Stern, N. (2006) Stern Review on the Economics of Climate Change, Cambridge. Full text available at: http://www.hm-treasury.gov.uk/independent_reviews_ index.cfm

Stole, I. (2006) 'Cause-related marketing': why social change and corporate profits don't mix, PR Watch: Centre for Media and Democracy, 14 July. Available at: http://www.prwatch.org/node/4965 (accessed July 2007).

Strasser, S. (1999) *Waste and Want: A Social History of Trash*. New York: Henry Holt.

Talen, B. (2003) *What Should I Do if Reverend Billy is in my Store?* New York: The New Press.

Teo, Hsu-Ming (2002) Wandering in the wake of empire: British travel and tourism in the post-imperial world, in S. Ward (ed.) *British Culture and the End of Empire*. Manchester: Manchester University Press.

Terranova, T. (1996) Digital Darwin: nature, evolution and control in the rhetoric of electronic communication, *New Formations* 29: 69–83.

Terranova, T. (2000) Free Labour: producing culture for the digital economy, *Social Text*, 18(2): 33–57.

Terranova, T. (2004) *Network Culture: Politics for the Information Age.* London: Pluto.

Theaker, A. (2002) *The Public Relations Handbook.* London: Routledge.

Thomas, L. (2008) 'Eco-reality': disquiet and desire in contemporary lifestyle television, *Cultural Studies* 22(5–6), forthcoming.

Thrift, N. (2006) Re-inventing invention: new tendencies in capitalist commodification, *Economy and Society*, 35(2): 279–306.

Timms, D. (2004) Personal communication with David Timms, Press Officer, World Development Movement.

Tisdall, S. (2007) First test for little big man, *The Guardian*, 7 June. Available at: http://www.guardian.co.uk/international/story/0,,2096965,00.html (accessed January 2008).

Toffler, A. (1980) *The Third Wave.* New York: Bantam Books.

Townsend, M. (2003) Oxfam bows to market and scraps fairtrade brand, *The Observer*, 19 January.

Townsend, M. (2005) Minute's silence to mark global death toll of hunger, *The Observer*, 29 May.

Turner, B. (2002) Cosmopolitan virtue, globalization and patriotism, *Theory, Culture & Society*, 19(1–2): 45–64.

United Nations (2007) The last stand of the orangutan – state of emergency: fire, illegal logging and palm oil in Indonesia's national parks. Available at: http://www.unep.org/grasp/docs/2007Jan-LastStand-of-Orangutan-report.pdf (accessed January 2008).

VanAlkemade, R. (dir) (2007) *What Would Jesus Buy?* USA: Warrior Poets.

Vanity Fair (2007) *The Green Issue.* April.

Venn, C. (2002) Altered states: post-enlightenment cosmopolitanism and transmodern socialities, *Theory, Culture & Society*, Special Issue on 'Cosmopolis', 19(1–2): 65–80.

Wainwright, H. (2003) *Reclaim the State: Adventures in Popular Democracy.* London: Verso.

Ware, V. (1992) *Beyond the Pale: White Women, Racism and History.* London: Verso.

Weber, M. ([1905] 2003) *The Protestant Ethic and the Spirit of Capitalism.* London: Dover Press.

Wernick, A. (1991) *Promotional Culture.* London: Sage.

White House (2007) Open Letter on the President's position on climate change, 7 February. Available at http://www.state.gov/g/oes/rls/or/80451.htm (accessed January 2008).

Williams, A. (2007) For sale: the virtues of ecology, *New York Times* extract in *The Observer*, 8 July.

Williams, R. (1989) *Resources of Hope: Culture, Democracy, Socialism*. London: Verso.

Williamson, J. (2002) An anti-capitalist Bildungsroman, *New Formations*, 45: 210–14.

Winship, J. (1980) Woman becomes an individual: femininity and consumption in women's magazines 1954–69, Stencilled Paper, CCCS. Birmingham: University of Birmingham.

Wintour, P. (2007) Ministers ordered to assess climate cost of all decisions, *The Guardian*, 22 December. Available at: http://www.guardian.co.uk/environment/2007/dec/22/climatechange.carbonemissions (accessed January 2008).

Wood, J. (2003) Make Trade Fair campaign: effective communications, in Global Action Plan (ed.) *Conference Summary* of the Consuming Passion Conference, December.

Woodhead, A. (2004) Telephone interview with Alison Woodhead from Make Trade Fair, Oxfam UK.

Wu, C. (2002) *Privatising Culture*. London: Verso.

Wyatt, S. (2005) *The People's Tycoon: Henry Ford and the American Century*. New York: Knopf.

Zick Varul, M. (2008) Consuming the campesino, *Cultural Studies*, 22(5–6), forthcoming.

Zylinska, J. (2005) *The Ethics of Cultural Studies*. London: Continuum.

Index

CITIZENS OR CONSUMERS?
What the Media Tell Us about Political Participation

Justin Lewis, Sanna Inthorn and Karin Wahl-Jorgensen

"In this superb account of how the British and American news media represent everyday citizens and public opinion, the authors show how coverage of politics and policy debates subtly – even inadvertently – urge people to see themselves as and thus to be politically passive, disengaged and cynical. The book's analysis of how journalists misrepresent, even invent, public opinion is alone worth the price of admission. Written with great verve, passion and unswerving clarity, Citizens or Consumers? promises to become an instant classic in the study of the failings–and the still untapped promise–of the news media to further democracy."

Susan J. Douglas, Catherine Neafie Kellogg Professor and Chair,
Department of Communication Studies, The University of Michigan

"Based on an exhaustive cross-Atlantic empirical study, Citizens or Consumers? is an engaging and incisive contribution to a subject usually restricted to clichés and vague generalizations. Looking not only at how media impact upon their audiences, but the manner in which that influence is mediated by the way in which citizenship itself is represented in news stories, Lewis et. al. offer us unusual and keen insight into a familiar world. Written in an engaging and lively style, first year students and experienced faculty members (as well as general readers) will benefit from its many perceptive insights. Especially useful are the last few pages which suggest how journalists might alter their representation practices to invoke citizenship rather than passive consumerism."

Sut Jhally Professor of Communication, University of Massachusetts at
Amherst Founder & Executive Director, Media Education Foundation

"The two great duelists for our attention – citizens and consumers – are locked in a struggle for the future of democracy. Citizens or Consumers? offers its readers a sharp lesson in how the media highlight and distort that struggle. It's the kind of lesson we all need."

Toby Miller, author of Cultural Citizenship

In recent years there has been much concern about the general decline in civic participation in both Britain and the United States – especially among young people. At the same time we have seen declining budgets for serious domestic and international news and current affairs amidst widespread accusations of a "dumbing down" in the coverage of public affairs. This book enters the debate by asking whether the news media have played a role in producing a passive citizenry. And, if so, what might be done about it?

Based on the largest study of the media coverage of public opinion and citizenship in Britain and the United States, this book argues that while most of us learn about politics and public affairs from the news media, we rarely see or read about examples of an active, engaged citizenry.

Key reading for students in media and cultural studies, politics and journalism studies.

Contents: *List of tables – Series editor's preface – Democracy, citizenship and the media – Meet the public – How active are citizens in the media? – Reporting opinion polls – The vox populi: Out of the mouths of babes and citizens – Talking about the public: Inferences about public opinion – Public opinion in crisis: September 11th and its aftermath – Getting engaged? – References – Index.*

2005   168pp

978-0-335-21555-3 (Paperback)

ORDINARY LIFESTYLES
Popular Media, Consumption and Taste

David Bell and Joanne Hollows (eds)

Lifestyle media – books, magazines, websites, radio and television shows that focus on topics such as cookery, gardening, travel and home improvement – have witnessed an explosion in recent years.

Ordinary Lifestyles explores how popular media texts bring ideas about taste and fashion to consumers, helping audiences to fashion their lifestyles as well as defining what constitutes an appropriate lifestyle for particular social groups. Contemporary examples are used throughout, including Martha Stewart, *House Doctor, What Not to Wear, You Are What You Eat, Country Living* and brochures for gay and lesbian holiday promotions.

The contributors show that watching make-over television or cooking from a celebrity chef's book are significant cultural practices, through which we work on our ideas about taste, status and identity. In opening up the complex processes which shape our taste and forge individual and collective identities, lifestyle media demand our serious attention, as well as our viewing, reading and listening pleasure.

Ordinary Lifestyles is essential reading for students on media and cultural studies courses, and for anyone intrigued by the influence of the media on our day-to-day lives.

Contributors: *David Bell, Manchester Metropolitan University; Frances Bonner, University of Queensland, Australia; Steven Brown, Loughborough University; Fan Carter, Kingston University; Stephen Duncombe, Gallatin School of New York University, USA; David Dunn; Johannah Fahey, Monash University, Australia; Elizabeth Bullen, Deakin University, Australia; Jane Kenway, Monash University, Australia; Robert Fish, University of Exeter; Danielle Gallegos, Murdoch University, Australia; Mark Gibson; David B. Goldstein, University of Tulsa, USA; Ruth Holliday, University of Leeds; Joanne Hollows, Nottingham Trent University; Felicity Newman; Tim O'Sullivan, De Montfort University; Elspeth Probyn; Rachel Russell, University of Sydney, Australia; Lisa Taylor; Melissa Tyler; Gregory Woods, Nottingham Trent University.*

2005 296pp
978-0-335-21550-8 (Paperback) 978-0-335-21551-5 (Hardback)

DOMESTIC CULTURES

Joanne Hollows

Although 'home' is central to most people's experience of everyday life, the meaning of home is often taken for granted. In this accessible and student-friendly introduction to domestic cultures, Joanne Hollows surveys current thinking and approaches to demonstrate why home is so central to our lives.

Domestic Cultures examines which meanings and values have been associated with home and demonstrates how these have been transformed and reworked in different historical contexts. The book shows that while certain meanings of domestic culture are frequently produced 'for us', these can be negotiated and resisted through everyday home-making practices. She demonstrates how elements of domesticity have been dislocated and mobilized within public life.

This wide-ranging text challenges a range of ideas about domestic culture. It examines how the meanings of domestic life are produced across a range of discourses and practices, from architecture, lifestyle media and advertising to home decoration, cooking and watching television. The book demonstrates how domestic cultures are not only linked to particular ideas about gendered identities, but how they are also differentiated by class, race and sexuality.

Domestic Cultures is a key introductory text for media, sociology and cultural studies students.

Contents: *Foreword – Acknowledgements – Introduction – Histories of Domestic Culture: Gender and domestic modernity – Home-centredness: Suburbia, privatization and class – Home-work: Feminisms, domesticity and domestic labour – Home-making: Domestic consumption and material culture – The media in domestic cultures – Dislocating public and private – Glossary – Bibliography – Index.*

2008 184pp
978-0-335-22253-7 (Paperback) 978-0-335-22254-4 (Hardback)

MUSEUMS, MEDIA AND CULTURAL THEORY

Michelle Henning

Museums can work to reproduce ideologies and confirm the existing order of things, or as instruments of social reform. Yet objects in museums can exceed their designated roles as documents or specimens. In this wide-ranging and original book, Michelle Henning explores how historical and contemporary museums and exhibitions restage the relationship between people and material things. In doing so, they become important sites for the development of new forms of experience, memory and knowledge.

Henning reveals how museums can be theorised as a form of media. She discusses both historical and contemporary examples, from cabinets of curiosity, through the avant-garde exhibition design of Lissitzy and Bayer; the experimental museums of Paul Otlet and Otto Neurath; to science centres; immersive and virtual museums; and major developments such as Guggenheim Bilbao, Tate Modern in London and the National Museum of the American Indian in Washington D.C.

Museums, Media and Cultural Theory is unique in its treatment of the museum as a media-form, and in its detailed and critical discussion of a wide range of display techniques. It is an indispensable introduction to some of the key ideas, texts and histories relevant to the museum in the 21st century.

2005 200pp
978-0-335-21419-8 (Paperback) 978-0-335-21420-4 (Hardback)

KEY ISSUES IN CRITICAL AND CULTURAL THEORY

Kate McGowan

"... the ideal book for students of cultural theory and one that is sensitively attuned to the political challenges of our times. Whether explaining dialectical materialism or the lyrics of Oasis and The Arctic Monkeys, Kate McGowan is an enlightening and entertaining guide."

Professor Stephen Regan, Durham University

From a man with electric underpants, to the indelible mark of 9/11 in a global cultural imaginary, Kate McGowan addresses the questions of cultural meaning and value which confront us all today. The book explores the often complex paradigms of critical thinking and discusses the possibilities of engaging and critiquing the cultural values that relate to our present.

Dealing directly with the issues entailed in cultural analysis, the book avoids simply looking at the eminent authors or movements in critical and cultural theory, and instead focuses on why studying culture matters to us today:

What are the 'proper' objects of cultural study?

What makes something 'art'?

What can critical and cultural theory contribute to contemporary debates about ethics?

What possibilities are opened up by theories of 'otherness' in thinking about the stranger or outsider in today's society?

How does a culture contest its own values – in relation to race, gender, class, sexuality and a variety of faiths and abilities?

Key Issues in Critical and Cultural Theory is key reading for students studying humanities, and for those with an interest in culture, aesthetics, ethics and philosophy who want to understand how these affect the world.

Contents: *Acknowledgements – Introduction – Textuality and Signification – Aesthetics – Ethics – Alterity – The Real – The Inhuman – Conclusion – Glossary – Notes – Bibliography.*

2007   176pp
978-0-335-21803-5 (Paperback)   978-0-335-21804-2 (Hardback)

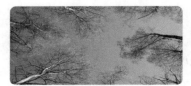